# Secrets of Academic Excellence

# Secrets of Academic Excellence

Methods of self-directed learning

Dr. Jaerock Lee

**Secrets of Academic Excellence** by Dr. Jaerock Lee
Published by Urim Books (Representative: Johnny H. Kim)
73, Yeouidaebang-ro 22-gil, Dongjak-gu, Seoul, Korea
www.urimbooks.com

All rights reserved. This book or parts thereof may not be reproduced in any form, stored in a retrieval system, or transmitted in any form or by any means, electronic, mechanical, photocopying, recording or otherwise, without prior written permission of the publisher.

Unless otherwise noted, all Scripture quotations are taken from the Holy Bible, NEW AMERICAN STANDARD BIBLE, ®, Copyright © 1960, 1962, 1963, 1968, 1971, 1972, 1973, 1975, 1977, 1995 by The Lockman Foundation. Used by permission.

Copyright © 2022 by Dr. Jaerock Lee
ISBN: 979-11-263-1014-2  03230
Translation Copyright © 2016 by Dr. Esther K. Chung. Used by permission.

Previously published into Korean in 2011 by Urim Books in Seoul, Korea

*First Published in September 2022*

Edited by Dr. Geumsun Vin
Designed by Editorial Bureau of Urim Books
For more information contact: urimbook@hotmail.com

# Introduction

Today we are in the midst of a flood of new information and knowledge that is being released daily. People study continually to acquire the knowledge just to survive the competition in today's world.

Not just those who strive to become experts in certain fields but also company employees or business people need to study if they want to succeed in the competitive markets.

Not even housewives are exceptions. They also have to study to make their lives more abundant or to help their children with their education. For this reason we hear the term 'lifelong education' more often than in the past. In this trend, there are also many self-improvement books being published.

During my ministry, I've seen many students who were worried about their future and their studies. Some of them consulted me because their grades were not going up even though they were trying hard. Some others consulted me because they could not really find a reason for studying and setting goals in life.

I prayed about these problems with the desire that the students should be able to excel in their studies and lead a successful life, giving glory to God. God answered me and gave me these messages on the secrets of academic excellence.

God is the origin of all knowledge and wisdom (Psalm 111:10; Proverbs 1:7, 9:10), and thus, the ways of studying that we get from Him would certainly be the most efficient. Learn these secrets of academic excellence given by God and find the best of the methods of studying for you personally. Furthermore, if you rely on the Holy Spirit, who knows you the best, you can also realize God's plan for you and have a clear goal in life.

The messages on the 'Secrets of Academic Excellence' are beneficial not only for students. They can benefit the parents who want to guide their children's education, and company employees or other professionals who desire to improve their skills. Above all, these messages are beneficial for our walk in faith. In order to fulfill our God-given duties in different areas, we need to improve our knowledge and skills. Once you learn these messages properly and apply them in your lives, you'd be able to accomplish any of your goals.

Basically, the same amount of time is given to everybody. A person's life will be different from the lives of others depending on what one does with that given time. God says in Ephesians 5:16, *"...making the most of your time, because the days are evil,"* and we must not waste any time. The lifetime given to Christians is the time given to prepare themselves as the brides of the Lord and to wait for Him who is coming again. Just as the most successful students seek to find the best method of learning and study hard, I hope you will apply these messages to your lives and strive to adorn yourselves as beautiful brides of the Lord.

If you do not know where to start, I urge you to set a goal both spiritually and physically, following the guidance of the Holy Spirit.

I convey my thanks to Geumsun Vin, the director of the editorial bureau of Manmin Central Church and her staff. I pray in the name of the Lord that all the readers might keep these secrets of academic excellence in their minds, achieve their goals, and become individuals who are acknowledged everywhere for acquiring, possessing and maintaining outstanding qualities of knowledge, skills and abilities.

October 2011
Dr. Jaerock Lee

# Contents

Introduction

## Part 1
## For Your Dream and Happiness · 1

Having a proper purpose
Seeking one's dreams
In order to set a career path
For your own happiness
Prepare for the future
Studying necessary for spiritual growth

In addition_The power of a dream and of a vision

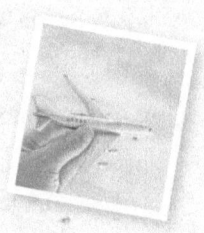

## Part 2
## How to Excel Academically without a High IQ · 21

Differences in learning abilities depending on IQ
Keys to getting good grades with an average IQ
Secret 1: Increase your IQ through spiritual methods.
Secret 2: Plow the field of your heart!
Secret 3: Develop your talents!

In addition_Attitude is more important than IQ

## Part 3
## Secret to Excel Academically in Unfavorable Circumstances • 41

Peaceful family
Home and school with atmosphere fit for studying
Other good surroundings
To achieve academic excellence in difficult situations
Joseph overcomes his circumstances

In addition_Relationship between parents and children

## Part 4
## Secret to Studying with Concentration • 63

Remove the source of idle thoughts
Categories of idle thoughts
Secret 1: Do away with environments that involve untruths.
Secret 2: Get rid of the untruths from your memory!
Secret 3: Make concentration a habit!
How to form the habit of studying

In addition_Addiction to TV and its withdrawal response

Part 5
# A Guide for Better Grades • 93

Secret 1: Enjoy your studying
Secret 2: Do the previews and reviews
Secret 3: Good life habits

In addition_21-day project for 'habit of success'


Part 6
# Studying with Heart • 119

Heart of good soil
Seeing with eyes of faith in everything
Do not stop until the goal is achieved
You can do more than with your own capabilities

In addition_Self-directed learning

- Part 1 -

# For Your Dream and Happiness

"The fear of the LORD is
the beginning of wisdom,
and the knowledge of the Holy One
is understanding."

Proverbs 9:10

An education commentator asked children, "Why do you study?" The most common response was because they were afraid of being punished. They study only because they feel coerced and have to do it. So, how boring studying would be for them! It is highly unlikely that they'd find studying interesting and fun.

<u>Studying is a price that one must pay to achieve his goals for a better future. So, isn't there a more enjoyable way to study?</u>

People start learning at birth. Little children in particular input a lot of information very fast like a sponge absorbs water. They never stop asking questions of their parents saying, "Mom, what is this?" "Dad, what is that?" "Why is the sky blue?" "Why do the birds chirp?" "Why can't puppies fly?"

For them everything in this world is a wonder and they want to know about everything. As in their case, the process of learning what we do not know in our lives is 'studying'.

Dictionary defines studying as "to apply one's mind purposefully to the acquisition of knowledge or understanding of (a subject)." We can also say that studying is the process of gathering information; analyze it; judge the plausibility of the information and input the information. It is even utilizing that knowledge in our lives. Through such a process, people can cultivate their personalities and become fully-functioning mature adults in the society.

## Having a proper purpose

In the past, there were people who studied to seek the truth and live a proper life. They sought answers to meaningful questions such as, "How can we live a life of truth and happiness?" and they studied to discover the answers. But as time passed, people's questions changed to become more like, "How can we live more comfortable and more materialistic lives?"

Nowadays, most students study hard to go to good colleges and get a job that pays well. The problem is that the gates to good colleges and well-paying jobs are small, and the competition is fierce. Competition in good faith can have positive consequences for everyone, but too much competition will have negative effects on the students. They feel that their studies are burdensome, and they begin to think of their friends only as competitors. In fact many students are suffering from the stress that comes from excessive competition.

Therefore, it is important to understand the purpose of studying. I said studying should be done for one's happiness. If the purpose of studying is limited to college entrance or getting a good job, there would be more of burden and pressure than the joy of studying itself.

Studying is a process to learn something we don't know. If we can find some kind of fun or joy in this process, it'd be much easier to study. Furthermore, if we have a clear reason for studying, we'd have different feelings toward studying. Then students will not study just because of their parents' coercion, but study in order to challenge the bigger world and achieve their dreams.

## Seeking one's dreams

By studying one can achieve his dreams more easily and he can have more opportunities. That is why many people study hard although it is something difficult. If they really understand that studying is a means to achieve their dreams they would have a different feeling about studying. They'd have the desire to study hard. Even if they have to reduce their sleep and give up so many other things just to study, they wouldn't feel it so hard. But rather, they'd find it fun to acquire new knowledge.

For example, if you have a clear goal to become a praise leader and give glory to God, you'd study singing, musical instruments, or dancing and improve your skills. Also, there are other students who study broadcasting, publishing, foreign language translation and interpretation, computers, photography, or graphic design to become experts in their field.

<u>In this way, if you have a clear goal, you wouldn't feel so burdened even if the studying is hard sometimes. You'd rather be filled with hope because you know that you are getting a step closer to your goal. Also, the more you study, the more confidence and sense of achievement you will get, and then you will try harder.</u>

After setting a dream and a goal in your life, you should also think about the details. For example, you should think about what you will major in, which college to attend and what kind of firm you would like to work for. In middle school you should have some idea about what you want to do with your life. By the time you are in high school it should

## Studying?

Studying is the driving force to challenge the world and achieve our dreams. Our feelings about studying will be different if we have a dream.

become much more refined and clearer. Just before the college entrance exam you should focus on specific subjects that are most needed. So, if you have a clear goal and a dream, you'd study by yourself without anybody's coercion.

It is of no use for the parents to tell their dreamless children, "Study hard, so you can get into a good college and become successful." They should first guide them to have a goal in their lives. Also, parents have to motivate their children to study by providing them with many opportunities to realize the importance of studying.

## In order to set a career path

In order to achieve your dreams you should also select a career path accordingly. During the school years you should find what kinds of talents you have and what you like doing. Some students have a clear goal and pursue it very well while other students have no idea what they want to do in the future.

In order to decide your future path you have to understand what you are interested in the most. If you are interested in something, it is likely that you are good at it. Most people like what they are good at.

If you sing well, write well, or excel in a particular sport, you might have a clue to what you are going to do in the future. If you are interested in cooking, fine art, machinery, science, or math, you might consider doing something that is related to such fields in the future. Even though you are not very talented in anything, you can develop your talents and skills if you focus on a particular field in which you are interested.

<u>Some think they do not excel in any area. But everybody has an interest in something. So, if such a person tries to look around a little harder they would probably be able to find their hidden talents.</u>

There was a student whose grades were at the bottom, but he got top marks in history. Others asked him how he got high marks only in history. He answered, "I came across a history book, and it was so interesting, like a children's story. I read history books every day after school. I read them so much that I could almost memorize them, but it was not boring." If you have anything that you can do with pleasure, it'd be easy to decide your career.

But realizing your talents or a field of interest does not mean your dream or goal is accomplished. You have to keep working on that area believing that God will help you accomplish your goals.

You have to study hard and put more focus on the field

that you'd like to have a career in. While doing all the academic work, you should get hands on practice in the area you are looking into as needed.

Yuna Kim, the figure skating Olympic gold medalist, had a dream to become an excellent skater like Michelle Kwan. Since she had somebody to look up to, she could try harder and her skills improved much faster.

But even though she had the talent, she still had to practice again and again until she could actually perform the higher level techniques skillfully. If she had given up only because she couldn't master the skills after a couple of tries, she wouldn't have been what she is today. Whenever she felt she was at a dead end she just pushed herself towards her goal, and finally she became an Olympic gold medalist.

Nothing is free in this world. You have to make it a habit to enjoy challenges together with the process of learning. Learning is necessary not only for students but for everybody. We all have to keep learning to achieve greater dreams.

## For your own happiness

As you acquire extensive knowledge and good manners through studying, you are likely to be given more career options. Studying can also help you to be acknowledged in society and lead to a happier life as well.

God wants us to be happy more than anybody else. That is why He said, *"...and to keep the LORD's commandments and His statutes which I am commanding you today for your good"* (Deuteronomy 10:13). Now, what could be the happiest thing for believers in the Lord?

It is to give glory to God in whatever we do. 1 Corinthians 10:31 says, *"Whether, then, you eat or drink or whatever you do, do all to the glory of God."* The purpose of studying lies here, too. If you study hard for the glory of God, He will certainly bless you. He will guide your path in your career selection and lead you to the best possible way.

Matthew 5:16 says, *"Let your light shine before men in such a way that they may see your good works, and glorify your Father who is in heaven."* If you, as a student, carry out all your duties and act responsibly while excelling in your studies, you will be a good example to many people.

If you also do better than what you could have done in your studies by receiving God's grace and strength, you can give glory to God through this. People around you will acknowledge God thinking you are able to study better because you are a believer.

You may not be able to get good grades right away. You may not immediately be able to give glory to God with your knowledge and talents. Nevertheless, if you just study hard,

God accepts it as glory in itself and He will lead you in the most prosperous way.

## Prepare for the future

Students cannot give a large amount of offerings or spend much time working for God like grown up adults. But if they do their best in their given positions in the church, such as being a class leader or a choir member, God will reward them with blessings.

But that does not mean you should neglect your studies and just spend all your time to fulfill church duties. It is the will of God that you study hard and prepare for the future when you are a student.

Ecclesiastes 3:1 says, *"There is an appointed time for everything. And there is a time for every event under heaven."* If the fruit is borne too early on a very young tree, the fruit is not good, and it is difficult for the tree to mature fully. The tree must first grow with firm roots, then branches and then many leaves. Only then will the fruits be good and they will not lay great burdens on the tree.

It's the same with the students. Now is the time for you to prepare to bear the fruit. You have to supply nourishment to your body to be healthy. You have to make your inner

Be happy

## My Happiness?

The greatest happiness for Christians is to give glory to God in whatever they do. If you understand why you need to study and do your whole duty as a student, God will be pleased with you and give you back blessings and rewards, making your life a valued life.

self mature, gain knowledge, and go through the process of gaining the kinds of experiences you need.

Along with this, you should also grow up in spirit through the word of God and prayer. Only when you prepare yourself both physically and spiritually can you form the strong wood that can be used as pillars in the kingdom of God.

When I preached the messages on the secrets of academic excellence, I talked about studying with heart. One of the students said he kept in mind that one needs to understand the general concept first and then focus on the details, and it was very effective for him.

He was one of the leaders in the Sunday school and went home late after the meeting was over. He had three subjects to study in the final exams the next day but he had not been able to study enough. To make things worse, there were some guests in his house and he couldn't really study.

He sat down at his desk at 11 PM after the guests were gone. But he became nervous because he felt the pressure that he had to study many subjects in a very short time.

At that time, he heard the voice from within his heart urging him to pray, and he prayed earnestly. As he began studying after the prayer, it was like his body and mind were being sucked into the book. He could remember the messages on the 'Secrets of Academic Excellence' and he could concentrate very well.

He could see which parts were the important parts, and the speed of learning became much faster. He could finish the studying within just one hour which ordinarily would have taken seven hours, and he did very well in the next day's exams.

There was another student whose grades were at the bottom of his class. He applied the messages on 'Secrets of Academic Excellence', and his grades went up to the mid-range and then to the top tier. Another student gave up going to college due to her low grades. But her grades went up within a short period of time after applying those messages, and she got into the college she wanted.

These messages can bring about good results not just for students' studying, but they can be applied equally to various kinds of exams, memorizing the Bible verses, and for general and technical reading. There is an elder in the church who is a police officer. When he was studying for the promotion exam he didn't have enough time for adequate preparation.

He couldn't even imagine passing the exam. But he listened to the 'Secrets of Academic Excellence' and he gained the confidence that he could do it. As he applied the messages, he got the highest marks in the exam.

Many people say they lack the ability or they are too old

when it comes to 'studying'. But whatever kind of life you've been living, it is all in the past. Anybody can start things anew including studying if he receives the strength of God.

It'd be one of the saddest of all things to have no dream or goal. Those who have goals in their lives are filled with energy and happiness. I hope you will also have a clear goal and dreams in the Lord.

## Studying necessary for spiritual growth

Studying is necessary not only for this earthly life but also for spiritual growth. Once we accept Jesus Christ and are born again as children of God, we are like spiritual toddlers. From this point in our lives, our faith has to grow to reach the full measure of the Christ by learning the Word of God. This is what a life of a Christian is supposed to be.

Just like students prepare themselves through studying, every believer is changed as true children of God in the process of leading their Christian lives. God created us to eternally share His love with us in the beautiful kingdom of heaven.

But because men were destined to fall into Hell due to their sins, God prepared Jesus Christ to open the way of salvation. Once we accept Jesus Christ and receive salvation, we can receive a more beautiful dwelling place in Heaven to the extent that we cast away sins and become holy through faith. God is cultivating mankind on this earth in order to gain holy and true children.

The Bible, which is the Word of God, is the written record about such heart and will of God in detail. It also gives us all the solutions to all kinds of life problems—the way to receive blessings, the way to receive eternal life, and the way to get true freedom.

If anybody takes delight in learning the Word of God and practices it, all things will prosper with him and he will be in good health even as his soul prospers (3 John 1:2).

<u>As explained, 'studying' is a must for all the aspects of our lives, both physical and spiritual. It is a way to learn all the secrets of the world and gain wisdom that we didn't have. Therefore, studying is something fun and joyous!</u>

> In addition

# The power of a dream and of a vision

In Japan, many people feed a colorful carp called Koi. This fish has a special trait. Koi living in river grows up to become 90cm-120cm but if they are put in an aquarium or a small pond, they grow up only as big as 15cm-25cm. In a fish bowl, they would grow up to only 5cm-8cm.

Just like Koi, whose size becomes very different depending on where they live, our lives can also become very different depending on the size of our dream and vision. The bigger the dream and the vision we have, the greater the person we can become.

Adolescence is the time when one needs dreams the most. An adolescent can study well if they have a dream. Having a dream can be very strong motivation to encourage people.

Soo Young Kim is the first student from a vocational high school who won in a TV quiz show of high school students. The following is what she said:

"In my teens, I wanted to get away from my poor family and suffocating school. I sometimes ran away from home and picked up drinking and smoking. I had to take a qualification exam (general equivalency diploma) for the middle school and went to Yeosoo Information Technology high school. And that school changed my life. There, I met a teacher who told me to have a dream. A while later, my life changed even more after seeing a photo in a newspaper. It was a Palestinian father who was crying with his little son in his arms who had been shot to death. My circumstances did not change at all, but my thoughts were changed as I had a dream. I picked up some books that my friends finished reading and studied them. Others told me I was not in a situation to go to a college, but I still had hope because I had a goal."

As she now had a dream, she concentrated on studying to become a reporter. In her first college entrance mock exam, she got 110 points out of 400, with which she couldn't get into any college. But after studying very hard, sleeping just 3-4 hours a day, she got accepted by Yonsei University, one of the most prestigious universities in South Korea, as an English major.

Those who have dreams become enabled to study hard. What kinds of dreams do you have? Why don't you imagine and write about your future?

- Part 2 -

# How to Excel Academically without a High IQ

"But the wisdom from above is first pure,
then peaceable, gentle, reasonable,
full of mercy and good fruits, unwavering,
without hypocrisy.
And the seed whose fruit is righteousness
is sown in peace by those who make peace."
-

James 3:17-18

At times believers consult with me about their children. They say, "My child is intelligent but does not study hard enough. What should I do about it?"

They think their children could do much better if they just tried but they lack the willpower to study hard. However, if you just scold them and force them to study, your actions are likely to bring adverse effects.

In order for your children to be able to get good grades, you have to first diagnose the situation. Medical doctors diagnose the patient before giving them any treatment or medicines. In the same way, if your children are not doing well, you should first find the reason and make appropriate changes.

<u>You cannot excel in your studies with your zeal only. There are conditions that need to be met. Among the conditions that must be met to excel in academics, let us first consider some of the conditions that are applicable to everybody. One of these is intellectual power.</u>

## Differences in learning abilities depending on IQ

In order to excel in academics, one needs appropriate intellectual power. Hearing this, is there anybody who is jumping to the conclusion thinking, 'Well, there isn't really any secret there! Those who are smart will get good grades, and since I'm not smart, I won't!'? If only those who are highly intellectual can get good grades, this book wouldn't be necessary.

The Intelligence Quotient is often referred to as the 'IQ'. It tells us about the functioning of the brain. Certain functions of the brain are measured and various ratings are assigned to them, and the result is the IQ. Comparing it with farming, the IQ is like a seed. If you sow the seeds of watermelon that is big and sweet, you are more likely to harvest sweet and large watermelons. If you sow seeds of watermelon that is small and not as sweet, the harvest is likely to yield such watermelons.

In genetics, they say that heredity factors count for 50% in part to the IQ. Namely, IQ is somewhat of an innate attribute. Just as it is likely that a good seed will bear good fruit, it is also likely that you will excel in your academics when you have an IQ that is higher than a certain level.

The IQ tests the following areas: memory power, numeracy, perceptive power, reasoning power, space perception, and the faculty of speech. All these abilities are just some parts of the brain's many functions, but they are absolutely necessary for studying. For this reason, if you have a higher IQ, you can expect that you should have higher learning skills.

So, most people would want their IQ or their children's IQ to be high. But not everybody can have high IQs. As the quality of the seeds from one watermelon to another is different, all people have different IQs. This contributes to people having different learning abilities.

Education scholars have categorized studying ability of children into 8 levels. The highest bracket, which is above 140, accounts for only 0.7% of the population, which is less than one person out of 100 people. The next bracket, from 130-139 is also a high level, which accounts for 2 or 3 out of 100. With this level of IQ, they should be able to receive a higher level of education than most other children.

The next bracket from 120-129 accounts for 7-8 out of 100, and they are relatively smarter than other children. 110-119 is mid-high level, which is a little better than the most common or average child. 90-109 accounts for the most children, about 46.8% of the whole population, which is the most common level of IQ. It is said that they are capable of the development of an intellectual level that is average or common in their age group.

From 80-89 is a little slower in the development of their intellectual level, but they have enough intellectual possibility to be better. 7-8 children out of 100 belong to 70-79 range, and they need special attention in their education. About 3 out of 100 belong to less than 70, and they have possibility of mental weakness, and they need the attention of experts. This is the categorization made by the experts on children, but we cannot say they are absolutely correct.

Nowadays, they have new ways to measure intellectual levels. Different testing methods and different countries have different ways of rating, so we cannot apply these kinds of figures to everybody. What we can understand for sure is that people have different learning skills according to the IQ.

### Keys to getting good grades with an average IQ

Though students attend the same class in the same classroom, some students understand the class very well while others can understand it only after learning it repeatedly. Those with good memory power will not forget the lesson though they attended just once. Other students tend to forget it easily. Among those who are in the same learning environment, those with higher IQ's are likely to do better in their studies.

Therefore, the parents should make demands of their children in accordance with their personal levels. If your child has a lower IQ or when they are a little slower in developing their intellectual power, you must not scold them saying they are not trying hard enough. You must not compare other children with your children either. They can develop a sense of inferiority, and they might come to hate studying.

<u>But this does not mean you should give up on your children because they don't have high IQs. You can assess the level of your children's learning abilities and encourage them and guide them step by step. Even if they are slow in learning, it can be accelerated and developed as they gain more and more confidence.</u>

## Secret 1: Increase your IQ through spiritual methods.

According to the research conducted by some scholars, you can increase your IQ to some extent. It can be increased during the growth stages. If children are provided with a good environment and education, some children's IQs can increase. But those students who are Christians can increase their IQ with spiritual methods. Since the IQ is the functioning of the brain, if you make your brain function well, you can increase your IQ.

It is the 'seed of life' that makes all our cells function normally. The seed of life is the trace of the breath of life that God breathed into Adam. The breath of life is of the original power of God.

Adam was created as a spiritual being and he received the breath of life from God. He was very wise because he was filled with the breath of life. Genesis 2:19 says, *"Out of the ground the LORD God formed every beast of the field and every bird of the sky, and brought them to the man to see what he would call them; and whatever the man called a living creature, that was its name."*

God created men with an exceptionally high intellectual ability. Even those scholars who devoted their whole life to studying animals are not able to memorize the millions of names and their traits. But Adam was so intellectual and he was wise enough to understand each animal's characteristics and give them names.

When he was living in the Garden of Eden the breath of life was passed down to his children automatically, but after he was driven out from there, it was not so. After the fall of Adam, most of his breath of life was taken away. When Adam was driven out to this earth from the Garden, the breath of life remained, but only a trace of it. This is the seed of life.

So, now because the seed of life is not passed down from parents to children automatically, God let the seed of life be put in the spirit of the fetus in the sixth month of pregnancy. At this time, the seed of life is not activated as if it were dormant. But when we accept Jesus Christ, the Holy Spirit comes into our heart and awakens this seed of life.

<u>Now, as we obey the commandments of God telling us to do, not do, keep, and cast away certain things, our heart will be filled with increasingly more truth. Then, the seed of life gains more strength and our spirit grows up. As the spirit grows up and if we become a man of spirit, all the body functions will be managed and controlled at the level of 'spirit'. The brain cells can also become more active, and one's learning ability will increase, too.</u>

Even though you are not a man of spirit, yet, the seed of life can function very well if you are filled with the Holy Spirit. In order to be filled with the Holy Spirit, above all, we must not have any barrier of sin between God and us. Also, we have to pray fervently.

The Holy Spirit can help us if we are full of the Holy Spirit. So, we can gain the faith that we can do the things that can never be done by human strength alone. If you cry out to God in prayer and begin studying, you can gain more power of concentration and you can cover a greater amount of material in a shorter time.

## Secret 2: Plow the field of your heart!

The second method to get good grades even with relatively low IQ is to make use of your IQ to the fullest by 'plowing' your heart.

Jesus compared the heart of men with 'field'. He categorized it into four types; roadside, rocky field, thorny field, and good soil. The roadside is a hardened heart that cannot understand or believe when they hear the Word of God. Those with rocky fields feel blessed when they hear the word, but they stumble in the face of trials or persecutions.

For those with thorny fields, the sprouts cannot grow up well because of the thorns. The thorns are the worries about the worldly things and desire and greed for secular benefits such as wealth, fame, and power. Those who have this kind of heart would think that they are living by the Word of God but they still suffer from various problems in family, money, or health. They can bear the fruit properly only when they get rid of the thorns from their hearts and practice the Word of God properly.

Good soil is the good field that is plowed well and that is

# Anybody can get good grades.

But, the wisdom of God should be sought.
When we fear God who is the origin of wisdom,
we can also possess excellent wisdom
and knowledge like Solomon did.

free of rocks and thorns. They can bear abundant fruit—30, 60, or even 100 times more than they sow. In a spiritual sense, it is the heart with which one can receive God's blessings because the person has cast off all untruths.

<u>For most people, their heart field is a mix of the four kinds of heart fields. Depending on what character is more dominant in one's heart, each one's heart becomes different. This in turn will bring about differences in their lives, especially in their walk of faith.</u>

Even the ordinary seeds, which are not the best of the quality, can produce good fruit if the farmer takes care of the crops very well after sowing them. The farmer can bring the best qualities out of the seeds that the seed is capable of producing. It is the same with the heart-field of men. You can pull out the best of your ability if you cultivate a good and sincere heart. Then, you can get good results.

Luke 8:15 says, *"But the seed in the good soil, these are the ones who have heard the word in an honest and good heart, and hold it fast, and bear fruit with perseverance."*

In fact, you don't have to have such a high IQ to get good grades. According to some research, many of those who are number 1 or 2 in each school had ordinary IQs.

A scholar named Lewis Terman observed children with

high IQs throughout their lives. He expected them to have great academic achievements and great success in the future. But the results were very different. Rather than those who had high achievements in studies and success in life, more of them had ordinary academic achievements and ordinary jobs.

Likewise, IQ is not the absolute determining factor in academic excellence. If you just have an ordinary IQ, that is, if the IQ is not extremely low, it is good enough to get good grades. As in farming, everything beyond the influence of the seed is decided by how good the field is and how diligent the farmer is. The same is true of the IQ.

No matter how smart one is, it is useless if he is lazy and does not try hard, or if his field of heart is barren. It might even become a disadvantage to that person. For example, some of those children with high IQs have no interest in their studies because they are bored and it's too easy, and they cannot adapt to the school life because they look down on education and other students.

Also, some of those who have high IQ concentrate on computer games and get addicted to them. Some people with high IQs try hard to become successful, but with that brain and position, they commit intellectual crimes. This is a result of having a good IQ, which is good seed, combined with bad heart-field.

For this reason, many in the fields of education talk about the importance of 'character' education. Other than IQ, they try to evaluate students with EQ (Emotional Quotient) and SQ (Spiritual Quotient).

It tells us that other factors than IQ play important roles in academic achievements and success in the society. EQ is the emotional quotient, and it is similar to the intelligence quotient of our mind.

What abilities does the EQ measure?

The first ability in measuring EQ is the ability to realize one's own feelings, and to respect them and accept them. Second is the ability to control one's impulses and other stressful feelings like nervousness and anger. Third is the ability to encourage oneself after a failure without getting discouraged.

Fourth is the ability to empathize with others' feelings. Fifth is the social ability to maintain harmony in a group and to cooperate with others. Details about these are explained in chapter 6, and you can refer to that later.

<u>If we cultivate our heart fields to make it 'good soil', EQ will increase. If we have high EQ, we will be able to control our mind, so we can drive away stress and idle thoughts. Even though your IQ is not very high, you can get good grades</u>

utilizing your IQ to the fullest degree, that is, if you plow your field of heart.

## Secret 3: Develop your talents!

If your children do not excel in academics such as mathematics or foreign languages, there are ways that will allow for them to gain an interest in those subjects. It is to let them learn those subjects through the things they like or what they are good at doing. Nowadays, they categorize men's intelligence in much broader detail in its measurement. It's because people have different strong points and weak points in their intelligence.

For example, there is a new concept called 'multiple intelligences'. The theory of multiple intelligences says that men's intelligence does not consist of IQ alone but also many other kinds of intelligences.

Howard Gardner, who created this theory, added the areas of bodily kinesthetic, musical, interpersonal, intrapersonal, and naturalistic intelligence to the conventional IQ ability consisting of linguistic, logical, mathematical and space perception abilities.

According to this theory, those who are good at sports have higher levels of bodily kinesthetic talent. Those who are interested in the living creatures like insects or birds have higher levels of naturalistic talent. According to this categorization, poor performance in languages or mathematics does not directly mean low intelligence. They can do other things comparatively better. If you find the things that the students are good at and encourage them to develop such abilities, the children can develop interest in their studies.

But some parents demand that their children strive to become a judge or a medical doctor in order to fulfill their own dreams. They try to take away the freedom from their children to choose their own career path. How hard would it be for the children if they do not want it, and if they don't have enough talent or giftedness to become what the parents demand of them?

But this does not mean if you are good at sports or performing arts, you don't have to study at all. Basic knowledge is necessary in all areas.

For example, you can communicate well with others with linguistic skills. Also, those who are interested in science can study more deeply when they have mathematical skills as well. Those who are studying performing arts can utilize their creativity more fully with knowledge in diversified areas. Above all, they can gain faithfulness and social skills while they go to school.

<u>Therefore, rather than studying only the subjects you like, it is wise to try one's best in all the other areas as well.</u>

Proverbs 9:10 says, *"The fear of the LORD is the beginning of wisdom, and the knowledge of the Holy One is understanding."* This is the profession that Solomon made in the inspiration of the Holy Spirit. Solomon offered a thousand sacrifices to God after he became the king.

*"God was very pleased with him and gave him wisdom as he wished. His wisdom surpassed the wisdom of all the sons of the east and all the wisdom of Egypt"* (1 Kings 4:29-30).

Wisdom comes from God. We can have excellent wisdom and knowledge like Solomon when we fear God who is the origin of all wisdom. To fear God is to shun evil, keep His commandments, and trust Him completely (Proverbs 8:13; 16:6).

If you revere God, you can recover the excellent ability given by God originally and excel in your academic affairs. I hope you will increase your intelligence by pleasing God and cultivate your heart into good soil to excel in your studies.

In addition

# Attitude is more important than IQ

The IQ test was devised by a French psychologist Alfred Binet in 1905 and was modified over the years. But Binet himself stressed the remarkable diversity of intelligence and the subsequent need to study it using qualitative, as opposed to quantitative, measures.

In 2003, the Korea Education Development Institute traced the outcomes of college entrance applications of the gifted children who were born around 1980. Unexpectedly most of them were accepted by mid-to-low class rated colleges. On the other hand, we can find that the world's leaders and intellectuals were made through their hardworking not just with innate intelligence.

What we should consider valuable is not just the IQ or giftedness but one's efforts. It is the effort to make something impossible take place; to overcome difficult situations; and to develop one's hidden abilities.

..................................................................................................
..................................................................................................
..................................................................................................

- Part 3 -

# Secret to Excel Academically in Unfavorable Circumstances

"Whether, then, you eat or drink or whatever you do,
do all to the glory of God."
-
1 Corinthians 10:31

There is a famous story about the mother of Mencius, a famous and great Chinese scholar. Mencius' mother moved her house three times for the sake of her son's education. Mencius was a Chinese Confucian philosopher during the Warring States Period. Mencius' father died early, and his mother raised him alone.

At first they were living next to a cemetery. And Mencius was imitating the paid mourners, because he didn't have friends to play with. Surprised, his mother decided to move. The next house was near a market in the town. Now, Mencius began to imitate the cries of the merchants, who were not respected in the society at the time.

So his mother moved to a house next to a school. From that time on Mencius began to read and learn about propriety, so his mother settled there. The mother's teachings and wisdom laid the foundation for Mencius to become a great scholar. What is the reason that this 2,000-year-old story is mentioned again and again today?

It's probably because what you see and hear as you grow

up is so important. So much so that the second secret of academic excellence is 'good environment'. Now, what kind of environment is necessary to succeed in academics?

## Peaceful family

The family is the most basic fence of protection that keeps the children safe. The family has to make the children feel safe and stable, so that they can focus on their studies. The most essential part in the formation of a good family environment is love and attention among the family members. For example, suppose there are always conflicts between the husband and wife or among the siblings. Then, to study in this environment is like studying on a battle field. Are there any parents who think, "We had an argument, but we didn't raise our voices." A war of nerves, namely a voiceless battle, is still a battle.

In childhood and adolescence, children are psychologically very sensitive. They are very sensitive about the mood of the family and they are easily affected by it. Wouldn't they know something is wrong when they see the dark faces of their parents? They would be nervous and worried knowing their parents had a fight.

Even though the parents do not quarrel, if they are too indifferent towards their children, it's not easy for the children to feel secure. For example, some parents just leave their children alone just because they are busy. Often the parents are absent from home and young children are left unattended in the house. In case of an only child, the child has to stay home alone.

Children become nervous when their parents are not home for a long time. They may also be exposed to TV or Internet without any protection. When both parents are working, many times it's not easy for them to give their children enough love and attention or spend quality time with them.

Some parents who have children in middle school or high school think that it's OK because the children are all grown up, but you shouldn't think so. Nowadays, they look all grown up, but it doesn't mean their inner-self is also mature. They are still immature in the ability to control themselves and make proper decisions for themselves. So, the parents have to help them.

It doesn't mean you should keep an eye on them 24 hours a day. Too much intervention will have negative effects. They might feel the interest of the parents too restrictive, and if they are constantly under the strict control of the parents, then they cannot become independent.

<u>The parents have to try their best within the given circumstances. The most important thing is that the children should feel that they are cared for and loved by their parents.</u>

There are those believing parents who might pray to God all the time and leave all circumstances of their children in God's hands. But, they should not think they did all their duty just by praying. Even though they are busy with other things, they have to take care of their children. They should see whether their children are doing well in their worship services and prayers; whether they are doing their homework well; whether they find a particular subject very difficult; whether they have a problem with any of their friends; or whether they have other troubles.

The parents could say something like, "I know it's hard to study. Let's just try a little more. Mom and dad will support you with prayers. Take a break to have some fruit." Or, "Is there anything mom and dad can do for you? You know you can always count on us." If they care for their children in this way, the children would be encouraged, feeling the love of their parents.

Proverbs 27:23 says, *"Know well the condition of your flocks, and pay attention to your herds."* When you care for even a pot of flowers or a little pet animal, how much do you

## Raising children

Even plants or animals grow better as you put in more effort. How much more would it be so with your children? Children are the souls entrusted to you by God, and you have to take good care of them both physically and spiritually.

have to care for them? They will grow well and healthy to the extent that you care for them. So how much more do you think you have to care for your children? You have to care for your children in spirit and body considering that each is a soul entrusted into your care by God.

You might not be able to spend a lot of time with your children, and you might not be able to provide them with enough financial support. However, you should try your best to let them feel your love, the love from your heart. Then, the children can feel secure within the fence of love and naturally be able to focus on their studies.

## Home and school with atmosphere fit for studying

Some parents tell their children to study but they themselves watch TV. Or, suppose family members talk and laugh loudly near the studying room. Then, what would the children feel when they're studying?

In such situations, the children who are studying will be distracted. Even though they are in the studying room, their mind will be outside, wondering what is on TV. Sometimes you think your children are too young to understand anything and just turn on the TV, but little children are affected by the TV even more than adults. They may even develop a love for watching TV as they grow up.

Instead of watching TV, if the parents read the Bible or other books and listen to sermons or praise songs, it will make a better atmosphere for studying. If the parents let the children have easy access to good books at home and also set a good example, they are likely to enjoy reading books as they grow up.

You should keep in mind that the children are a reflection of their parents. Of course, the students should also try not to come into contact with things that can distract or disturb them while studying.

Other circumstances outside of the family are also important. Schools are the place where students spend most of their time. If most students in a certain school generally study hard, your child will probably also study hard. If they have good friends around them, they can get help from them, too. It is beneficial to have friends who can study with you, who can share methods of studying, and who can teach and answer questions with kindness.

<u>There was a boy who was in the lowest quartile ranking in his school, but he began to study in the $10^{th}$ grade. The event that changed him was the change of his friends.</u>

He used to play computer games with his friends, but

those friends began to study in libraries or private institutions. Soon, he felt he couldn't live like he had been living any more either.

So, he also began to study hard. Initially he found studying difficult, but he followed the example of the number one student in his class. As a result, his grades went up so much that he was accepted by Seoul National University.

Along with friends, teachers can play a very important role. If you have teachers who give you hope, praise your good points and encourage you, you are likely to excel in studies.

You can understand this from the fact that if the students like certain teachers, they tend to get good grades in those teachers' subjects. In case of company employees, if your company always encourages the employees to study and improve their skills, and all the employees do so, you would also probably study hard. But if everyone around you is satisfied with the current situation, you are likely to join them and no longer try.

## Other good surroundings

The town where you live and the people you meet are also important factors for learning. Mencius' mother realized this fact from her experiences and moved to a good place.

One of the environments that believing students have

is the church. So, our church always tries to provide a good environment for them to study well while they lead a good life in faith as well.

For this reason we open English and math classes during every vacation. We try to create the environment that encourages students to study hard. If you try your best to learn the Word of God and pray hard, it is also creating a good environment for the students.

If a parent earns recognition in the workplace or company, it can also motivate the children. If the parent encourages and prays for the child who studies hard, they will feel much more strengthened. It is everyone's duty to create a good environment for the students.

Hearing this, do any of you think, "I don't have good family environment, school, and other circumstances, so what should I do?" Of course, it is good to have a better environment, but the environment is not the sole factor in academic excellence. Also, it's not easy to find a student who has a good environment in every aspect. For instance, a student may not have a good family environment, or he might have parents who are not believers.

<u>Now, in the case where it's not easy to change your unfavorable circumstances, what do you have to do? You can overcome your unfavorable circumstances.</u>

There are myriads of people who overcame difficult situations and achieved success in their respective areas. Ki Moon Ban, the Former Secretary General of the U.N., is a good example of a person who overcame the difficulties in his life. He went to elementary school right after the Korean War, and he had to study in a tent without proper desks or chairs. He was just a little boy in a poor country that had been swept by the waves of war.

But seeing the foreigners who came to aid South Korea, he began to have curiosity about the big world. He wanted to study English, but there were no textbooks. But he just learned the language by himself.

Eventually, he got a chance to study in the United States, which was not something easy for a boy from the countryside. During his stay in the United States, President Kennedy asked him what he wanted to be. He confidently said he wanted to be a diplomat. This short meeting with the President of the United States gave him great encouragement to fulfill his dream.

As he had many siblings, he had to study in a room full of his younger siblings. When the parents were busy, he had to chop the firewood, feed the pigs, or take care of his younger siblings. And yet he didn't complain but enjoyed studying and he thought about his parents who were also working so hard. All his efforts paid off. He finally was accepted by Seoul

## Further and higher

That which disturbs studying is not the environment.
It is actually the mindset
that makes you submit to the circumstances.
If you rely on God with faith you can overcome
the circumstances and go further and higher.

National University in political science and diplomacy major.

The experiences he had in his difficult situations served as nutrients that helped him develop wisdom and leadership. Such an unfavorable environment made him try harder and he humbled himself more. Many people wanted to help him when he was a diplomat because he was passionate, yet humble. Eventually he was elected as the Secretary General of the U.N. He was a leader who contributed to global peace significantly.

<u>Anybody can follow his example. If you are in a difficult situation, consider it as a good environment that makes you a better and deeper person. And as you try your best in the given circumstances, God will also help you according to your faith.</u>

## To achieve academic excellence in difficult situations

The thing that disturbs your studies is not the circumstances themselves. In fact, it is more your mindset that causes you to complain and submit to your circumstances. If you rely on God with faith, you can overcome the high waves or difficult situations. Instead of floundering, you can rise up to new heights using those high waves.

In particular, those of you who are believers in God can find it easier to rule over your circumstances. You can conquer and subdue your situations in reality with faith and the strength of God.

Let me briefly explain the spiritual principle applied here. The principle here is that the spiritual realm rules over the physical realm.

Your environment belongs to the physical space. Since spirit is in a higher dimension than flesh, if you stay in the spiritual space by faith, you can rule over the physical space. This faith will be given by God when we practice the words in the Bible. If we have this faith, we can gain the confidence to do the things that are impossible for men.

Mostly people find it difficult to study hard in a noisy place filled with commotion. Suppose you try to study but you hear some noise of fighting right outside. Or, telephone bells keep on ringing, or some unexpected guests distract you. Of course, some people try to overcome such circumstances with their mental power, but it's not something that's easy.

<u>But it is different for those who control their circumstances with faith. With the help of the Holy Spirit, they can overcome the limitations of men. Being in a very noisy environment, if they pray shortly, God will give them the strength to concentrate, so they can just ignore the noises</u>

<u>and focus on their studies. The noisy circumstances wouldn't matter to them because they can control their environments with faith.</u>

Sometimes, students might have to study in a place that is not really suitable for studying. For example, those who have part time jobs or those who have to practice their skills along with the studies do not have enough time to study.

So, they have to study during breaks in school or while they are moving by public transportation. But if they control the environment with faith, they can focus on their studies wherever they are. They can control their senses of hearing and seeing as they want.

<u>Furthermore, you can also control emotional environments. It's because those who can control their environments can also control their minds.</u>

For example, let's say your parents quarrel often, they are too busy to pay enough attention to you, or you don't have the money to buy all the things necessary for study or to get tuition for private education. If you are controlled by such circumstances, you wouldn't have willingness to study. You would only have negative thoughts thinking, "Why are my parents and my family like this? What's the use of studying anyway?"

But if you can control your mind with faith, you'd have thoughts in goodness. 'My parents are doing their best. It must be so hard for them, too! I will be their strength and joy by studying hard.' You wouldn't put the blame on the environment or your parents but you'd try your best to please your parents.

If you have to work at part time jobs to pay for your tuition or your living expenses while pursuing your studies why don't you make a positive remark with faith? "I am thankful that I can learn to be independent at such an early age! I think I have a big vessel since I am helping my parents! How lovely will I look in the eyes of God?"

## Joseph overcomes his circumstances

Among the patriarchs of faith we can see that virtually nobody came up in a good environment. God chose His people from the furnace of sufferings which were very difficult for men to overcome. And, He did the things in their lives that were possible only with God's power. One of the good examples is Joseph.

Joseph lost his mother at a young age, and he was separated from his father at the age of 17. His brothers hated him because their father showed favoritism to Joseph, and they eventually sold him to Midianite traders as a slave. Now he had to live as a slave at the house of Potiphar, the captain of the bodyguard in Egypt.

But he did not resent his circumstances or complain against God because of it. He just did his best in his duties, and God was with him. His master acknowledged him and made him the overseer over his house.

And yet there waited another hardship for him. By the groundless accusation of his master's wife, he was put into a jail where king's prisoners were held.

There he happened to interpret with the wisdom of God the dreams of two officials of Pharaoh, and two years later, this gave him a chance to interpret a dream that Pharaoh had. He did not only give the Pharaoh the interpretation of the dream but also the solutions to the problems, and Pharaoh made him the prime minister.

Joseph's early life was not a failure but a training course that God prepared for him. It let him gain what it takes to be the prime minister. His course was so hard that ordinary people would have been disheartened and given up in everything. But Joseph overcame everything. How? He had the dream given by God, and he had faith enough to try his best in everything despite unfavorable situations.

Secular people rely on and boast of their friends, wealth,

social power, or other backgrounds they have. But Psalm 20:7 says, *"Some boast in chariots and some in horses, but we will boast in the name of the LORD, our God."* As said, God will back us up if we rely on Him and boast in Him.

Even though we are in a difficult situation like that of Joseph, we should be encouraged knowing God the Father is with us. With the eyes of faith, unfavorable circumstances are a route to blessings that train us in various ways. I hope you will focus on your studies even though your circumstances are not favorable.

> In addition

# Relationship between parents and children

When a normal relationship between parents and a child is not properly formed and nurtured, the child may lack confidence and become easily discouraged when challenged. Keep in mind that the abilities formed at the early stage of children's life may change the course of their entire life and try to leave positive and good effect on your children.

Let us suppose there are two kinds of families as follows:

\<Jimmy's family\>
Mother: Jimmy, why are you playing video games all day? When are you going to study? I don't know what will become of you later! What will your younger brother learn from you?
Jimmy: I said I will play just a little bit! I don't want to talk to you!

\<Brian's Family\>
Mother: Have you been on the computer all night? I am worried that you play computer games too much. Wouldn't it be better if you can control yourself without me having to tell you to stop?
Brian: OK, I'll try to reduce the playing time. I know I play

games a little too much. I thought I was going to play just a little more but I lost the track of time. If I make a time table or plan, do you think I will be able to keep it?

More often many families talk like in the case of Jimmy's family. In this case the parents should check if they have a communication problem before they point their fingers at their children.

The basic element of conversation is 'respect' and 'empathy'. If the parents accuse their children, the children would only try to defend themselves in anger or sadness, rather than realizing their faults. The children would acknowledge their mistakes and accept their parents' advice only when the parents respect them as another human being when they try to talk with them.

Even when the parents have to discipline their children, it'd be much easier to continue the conversation if they begin with such remarks as, "I understand you are angry," or "Now I see what happened that day." Parents should make sure their children feel they are understood. Then the parents can present what they want from their children after explaining their viewpoint and their situations. The children would probably realize what they have to do by themselves.

And it'd be desirable to commend them when the children are trying to correct their behaviors. But unconditional praises wouldn't help the children. The commendation or compliment should be specific. It is better to say something like, "I am happy that you are trying to get up early by yourself!"

- Part 4 -

# Secret to Studying with Concentration

"For the mind set on the flesh is death,
but the mind set on the Spirit is life and peace."
-
Romans 8:6

Have you ever looked at the clock and suddenly realized that a considerable length of time had passed by without noticing it? This might mean that you regret having wasted a lot of time without getting much done. Or, it might mean that you lost the track of time because you were studying or working very hard.

In which situation do you usually find yourself? If you are always doing something but without much achievement, then it's probably because you lack concentration.

With increased power to concentrate, you can be absorbed in your work to the point that you will lose the track of time. If you focus the sunshine through a magnifying glass, you can even burn a piece of paper. Men's concentration can also have such great power.

The power of concentration will bring out the potentials that God planted in us. We can even be the best in our respective field if we can maximize such potentials.

Therefore, the third condition necessary to excel in academics is the power to concentrate on your studies.

## Remove the source of idle thoughts

Idle thoughts are various kinds of unnecessary thoughts. They disturb your studying. Students might have idle thoughts or daydream about the fun things that they can do with their friends, news about celebrities, or their boyfriends or girlfriends. Grown-ups may also have concentration disrupted due to thoughts about their job, family matters, or financial problems.

If you try not to have idle thoughts, more of them come to your mind! You might be trying to study, but your mind is full of other things. Thoughts after thoughts come to you mind: 'Where will I hang around with my friends tomorrow? Should I go to the rock concert or not? If I go, then what should I wear? Where should I meet my friends?'

Even though you sit at your desk for a long time, you cannot get good grades if you do not concentrate. Also, whether it is studying or doing your work, if you concentrate you can finish a certain work in a day, but having idle thoughts it takes a couple of days. How inefficient it is! If you study with idle thoughts, it is meaningless. It is just like shooting a bunch of arrows that never hit the target!

<u>Then, how can you drive away such idle thoughts, which are not even visible? First, you have to recognize the origin of</u>

such idle thoughts and remove it. Then, you can increase your concentration and use your time efficiently.

Idle thoughts keep on coming into your mind even though you try not to have them. It is because the things that you have seen and heard had already been input into your memory together with feelings about them.

For a better understanding, let's think about what 'thought' is. There is a memory device in the brain of a man. What you see and hear as you grow and mature will be stored along with feelings as 'knowledge' in this memory device. When this knowledge is retrieved, it is called 'thought'. As long as you have knowledge in the memory device, it can be retrieved as thought when that knowledge comes in contact with a stimulus.

If you type the word 'apple' into a search engine on the Internet, many different kinds of information about 'apple' will be shown. The memory device of our brain is similar. If you see an apple by chance, you will be reminded of the things about an apple that you have stored. When a piece of information is put into the memory, your feelings about it has the main effect on the formation of a memory.

Especially, the things of the world are usually provocative and sensual, so it is likely that you will have strong feelings about them when you see or hear about them. Then, it is easy for those things to be stored in your memory. Here, 'the things of the world' refer to all kinds of untruths that have nothing to do with God. They are hatred, argument, adultery, terror, hot-temper, arrogance, and so many others. If these things are input in the memory with strong feelings, they will be rooted deep inside the memory and last a long time.

When you transplant the rice seedlings in the rice paddy, they will fail in the water if you do not plant them deep enough. However, if you plant them deep enough, they can take root and grow well. In the same way, if what you see or hear is planted without strong feelings, it is not planted deep in your memory, and the memory goes away after a couple of days.

<u>But the knowledge that is planted with strong feelings deep within the memory will last longer. This 'feeling' plays a key role of planting the knowledge deep inside the memory device.</u>

If you experienced a house fire at a very young age, you will never be able to forget it for the rest of your life. You will clearly remember the weather conditions, what clothes you were wearing, or how people acted on that day. You remember it as if it happened just yesterday. You might think you forgot about it, but if you come in contact with anything that is related with that incident, you are reminded of it.

In this regard, those who experienced mentally shocking things like war, torture, natural disasters or other accidents are likely to suffer from PTSD (Post Traumatic Stress Disorder). It is a mental disorder in which one experiences the shock of that particular incident over and again to the extent that daily activities may be disturbed.

On the other hand, if you did not have any particular feeling when you came in contact with something of the world, you would soon forget what you saw or heard. But if you had some strong feelings coupled with something, you will keep it more deeply, and you will remember it well quite easily.

Also, the brain function of the students is very active, and they have better memories than adults. So, it is likely that they will be reminded of the things they have input with certain feelings better than older adults. Now, let us delve into some of the kinds of idle thoughts.

## Categories of idle thoughts

### Curiosity towards untruthful things of this world

Curiosity is a desire that is drawn towards new and out of the ordinary things. Students are going through a time when they have a lot of curiosity. There are many things in this world that they experience for the first time and that they find exciting. The curiosity itself is not something bad. The problem is they have curiosity that is directed towards the untruthful things of the world.

1 John 2:15-16 says, *"Do not love the world nor the things in the world. If anyone loves the world, the love of the Father is not in him. For all that is in the world, the lust of the flesh and the lust of the eyes and the boastful pride of life, is not from the Father, but is from the world."*

'The lust of the flesh', simply put, is the desire that causes us to commit sins. When people come in contact with an environment or the conditions suitable to commit sins, most of them have the desire to act out untruths such as hatred, envy, or various forms of sexual misconduct, and, their lust of the flesh will be revealed.

'The lust of the eyes' is one's heart being agitated by seeing or hearing things of the untruth together with the desire to seek those things. 'The boastful pride of life' is the desire to boast of oneself and follow the pleasures of the world. To sum it up, the source of idle thoughts is the world of untruth and not the truth.

For example, suppose a student watched a scene in a movie where lovers are deeply passionate. It was for the first time in his life he had seen such a thing. He is amazed. Later, the memory of that scene comes to mind while in class and during

## Strong feeling

Whether good or bad,
if you have a sensational
and shocking feeling
in an incident, it may be
distinctly engraved
into your memory
and trigger your idle thoughts.

his study time. His curiosity is stimulated and he thinks, "What kind of feeling would I have if I did it?"

<u>If you have curiosity about untruthful things, Satan will not miss that chance. Though invisible, there is the world of evil spirits, and the evil spirits try to control men's thoughts. They will come into your thoughts and stimulate and incite the desiresof the flesh and curiosity.</u>

Then, to fulfill that curiosity, you might look for and see similar kinds of movies. Your curiosity keeps on increasing, and you eventually develop a strong desire to date somebody and actually do those things.

Furthermore, just as climbing vines keep branching and growing, other idle thoughts keep coming to your mind. You will have thoughts like, "If I put on a nice outfit like a movie star, I can get a lot of attention. Where can I get those clothes? Do I also have to work out to have a better body?" Then, your mind and thoughts will be farther and farther away from studying.

Also, those who have experienced some physical contact with opposite sex will be reminded of their experience when they see anything similar. Then, they will have a strong desire to have the same kind of feelings once again.

The magnitude of feelings will vary depending on the age

of having such an experience. Children of different ages have different feelings about the same thing. As their bodies and mental age are more mature, they will have stronger feelings.

Also, even though they were too young to feel something significant at that time, they will have curiosity later, when they grow up to some extent. If they cannot overcome such curiosity and desire, they might do things that students are not supposed to do, or they might even commit crimes. Some children come in contact with adult movies in elementary school, and they continue to increase their curiosity and finally commit sins in their teens.

I hope you will realize that curiosity towards the untruthful things of the world will give rise to idle thoughts. Do not be deceived by Satan! He tempts you saying that taking the worldly things is good and entertaining, but it is a lie.

You might get pleasure for a moment if you subject yourself to the worldly things, but in the end you will be left with only a sense of vanity. You might also fall into eternal death. Therefore, if curiosity towards the worldly things arises, I hope you will drive it away thinking about the fearfulness of Hell, if it helps.

### Seeking secular pleasure

The desire to seek worldly pleasure will be stronger if you

feel studying is boring. This kind of idle thought is caused by the desire to seek the pleasures and fun that is of the world.

For example, those who really like computer games want to feel the pleasure of playing the game again and again. In more serious cases, the letters in the books look like an enemy that they have to destroy. They think of their study room as a space found in the game.

For some students, their minds are filled with hanging out with their friends. They have constant idle thoughts such as, "My friend and I are going to see a movie tomorrow! I want tomorrow to come quickly! He is going to treat me to the movie, so I wonder if I should buy dinner! What would we eat? How am I going to get the money?"

They soon begin to daydream without even studying one page of the book. They just cannot concentrate. Now you understand the cause of idle thoughts, so if you are spending your study time this way, you should drive them away. Then, you can just believe in yourself and concentrate without giving up.

**Untruthful feelings**

Some people lose the peace of mind and have idle thoughts because of untruthful emotions. For example, suppose your best friend suddenly stops talking to you, and she only hangs around with other friends.

You think like, "What is going on with her? Is she mad at me? How can she do that to me? She was whispering something to another girl looking at me, and she must have said something bad about me." You get a headache, and the contents of the book you are reading will not be remembered at all. Or, even if you are working with your computer, you cannot accomplish anything.

In fact, you are worried about something that is not even a certainty. You are also judging your friend.

Also, some students quarrel with their parents before they study. Eventually, they sit at the desk because their parents force them to, but they keep on having thoughts of complaints towards their parents. All the untruthful emotions such as hatred, complaints, and resentment are giving birth to idle thoughts like, "Why does mom always talk about studying? Why does she have to do it so often? She doesn't try to understand me."

The above things are some of the main kinds of idle thoughts, and now let us delve into what you have to do to remove them.

## Secret 1: Do away with environments that involve untruths

The source of idle thoughts is, after all, the knowledge and feeling of untruth. Therefore, if you cast off all untruths from your heart, you can get rid of all idle thoughts completely. But even though you are still in the process of changing, you can block the idle thoughts to the extent that you remove the knowledge and feelings of untruth from your memory.

Even though you get rid of untruths from yourself, it is useless if you keep on inputting untruth in you. You can purify your heart only when you do not see, hear, or speak anything that is of untruth. Otherwise, it will be useless even if you pray for 10 or 20 years. It means you just repeat the meaningless cycle of removing and then filling up the untruths in you again and again.

For some people, if they hear others whispering, they try to find out what they are saying. The desire to hear such gossip is evil in itself. In this regard, you have to keep away from those people who gossip.

Those who are good-hearted, they do not want to hear about other people's faults or other kinds of evil words. Because we cannot just close eyes and ears all the time, we cannot avoid coming in contact with evil things of the world completely. However, we still have to try our best to keep ourselves away from such things.

<u>Nowadays, the two major channels of untruthful things coming into you are TV and computers. So, if you just keep away from these two things, the amount of untruths in your memory will be reduced significantly.</u>

Of course, there are some good and educational TV shows, too. But there are far more shows for entertainment. They also show the things that can catch the eyes of people to increase their viewership. Then, if they go to the extreme, the contents become suggestive and provocative.

Some people even call TV the boob tube or idiot box because it is so unbeneficial. They say if you watch TV too much, your thinking ability will not develop. Also, watching TV is not good for the health of little children and teenagers who are growing up. Their eyesight will become bad, and if they are exposed to electromagnetic waves of the TV too much, they might have precocious puberty at the age of 7-8.

Computers are in many ways harmful, too. You can use it for Internet classes or for an encyclopedia, but there are a lot more things that are untruth. If you cannot keep your heart, it is better not to use it at all.

If you have to use it for homework, you should use it in the presence of your parents. You can also use other materials that are substitutes for computers, such as newspapers or books. Of course, life can be quite inconvenient if you do not use computers nowadays.

So, I hope you students will quickly gain the ability to control your minds. Then, you can use the computers only for good purposes.

In order to stop inputting any more untruths, other than trying to minimize the TV and Internet use, you should also try to have only good friends.

It's because in many cases you come in contact with untruths through your friends. And, so, it would be desirable if you can lead sound and healthy fellowship together with your friends. Also, when you take a rest after studying for a while, you should avoid Internet PC rooms or some streets that have adult entertainment. Instead, you can visit parks, museums, or art galleries where you can come in contact with nature and learn many good things.

In order to cut off idle thoughts you need to have determination to cut off input of untruths. You can also ask your parents to help you if you find it too difficult to control your mind by yourself in certain situations or conditions.

You can also ask God for His grace and strength by praying earnestly and fasting. God will surely help you. If you receive the fullness of the Spirit, you will gain the power to control yourself, and your desire for worldly things will decrease.

## Determination and effort

Just as we have to remove the pollutants to purify water,
we need the determination and effort to cut off the untruths
in order to block idle thoughts.
Along with this, if we change our thoughts and feelings into
those belonging to the truth and fill ourselves
with the words of God,
we can focus on studies without having idle thoughts.

## Secret 2: Get rid of the untruths from your memory!

Sometimes the things that you once saw and enjoyed may come back to your memory while you are studying. You do not actually accept any more untruths, but you still have untruths remaining that had been previously input. Now, you don't have to be disconcerted or discouraged, but you can just start erasing those things one by one.

When they purify a polluted river, how do they do it? First, they block the flow of the dirty water from coming into the river. Then, they remove the pollutants.

Moreover, they add clean water and oxygen by planting grasses that help with the purification. If we purify our memory in the same way, it will finally be cleaned.

We first block the untruths, and then we can begin to remove the untruths one by one that had already been input. No matter how much untruth you throw away, you cannot purify yourself as long as you keep on accepting untruths. Even if you try to cast away untruths by fasting and all-night prayers, it is of no use if you watch inappropriate TV shows or movies. You can cast away untruths only when you stop seeing, hearing, and accepting things of untruth.

Furthermore, as we fill our memory with the knowledge of truth, it can be purified more quickly. Your head will be cleared, and you won't have any more idle thoughts when you listen to sermons and learn the word of God.

<u>But the knowledge of untruth that is in your memory cannot be erased like a computer file you can easily delete. Then, what do you have to do? You have to change the thoughts and feelings. Then, the knowledge of untruth will become increasingly dim.</u>

Nowadays young students come in contact with many untruthful things on TV and the Internet. Companies release countless products and commercials related to sex. TV dramas or movies describe unfaithfulness as something romantic. Also, the overly exposed bodies of actresses or singers is referred in the media as being 'beautiful' and 'gorgeous'.

Young children whose values have not yet been firmly formed and who are raised in this kind of world might develop a distorted understanding and concept of sex. They look at the opposite sex as an object of lust. They might accept sexually extreme things that they see.

Moreover, they are supposed to dislike and hate sins, but instead they accept them as being something beautiful and good. They don't consider sins to be sins. Inappropriate knowledge and feelings about sex give rise to curiosity or lust.

1 Timothy 5:2 says, *"...the older women as mothers, and the younger women as sisters, in all purity."* It tells us that you should treat older women in the church as your own mothers and young women as your own sisters, in all purity. As written, boys should regard friends of opposite sex just as though they were your sisters who are born of the same parents, in all purity.

Also, you should consider the lust towards opposite sex to be as dirty and horrible as cockroaches or maggots in Hell. This is not an exaggeration.

In fact, lust and carnal pleasure are the main causes of leading the souls to death. Also, lust and pleasure are like thieves that steal time for studying and destroy precious dreams. Therefore, I hope you will always be on the alert and change your wrong feelings and thoughts about untruthful things.

**Secret 3: Make concentration a habit!**

Anybody can have a great concentration when they do something they like and it is enjoyable for them. If they liked a movie, it is likely that they can remember the name of the hero/heroin and tell others the whole story. It's because they concentrated on the movie.

Those who have already developed a good habit of

studying can concentrate on their studies for many hours when they want to. But for some other students, they feel it difficult to just sit down in study even for a short while. Some students begin their studies but give up mid-way because they haven't developed a good habit of studying. If you belong to this category, I suggest that you study regularly every day for a couple of weeks.

Though varied from person to person, it usually takes 14 days for a person to form a habit. Therefore, you should never give up mid-way thinking you can't do it before at least a couple of weeks have passed.

It is important to practice desired behavior every day. If you practice sitting down in study even for a short while for two whole weeks, then you will begin to develop a good habit of studying. As time passes, you will have more concentration power and will be able to enjoy studying. If you make it a habit to sit in one place and concentrate on your studies, it will be much easier to study.

## How to form the habit of studying

Did any of you give up studying thinking that you lack the basics and your grades are at the bottom? If they just try to do it, anyone can do well with the power given by the Lord (Philippians 4:13). Even if you lost your way during the puberty and missed out on school study time, or even if you lack the basic knowledge needed, you can just acquire studying methods that suit you the best.

### Tidying up the environment

Now, for you to actually develop a good habit of studying, let's go into your studying room. First, you should clean your room and straighten up your desk first. If things are lying around here and there, they will disturb you and distract you from concentrating. It is also good to remove the things that you touch or see often. The cell phone is the number one object to remove from your sight!

There is research conducted by Dr. Glenn Wilson of University of London, on the effects that the signal of arrival of electric information has on processing the information.

It says while doing a certain work, if you hear the sound of the arrival of a text message, check it, and reply, the intelligent quotient drops by about 10 points. In case of elementary school students, if they check or reply to the text messages in the middle of studying, it takes an average 5 minutes for them to re-focus on their studies.

Depending on the contents of the text messages, it might take 10 minutes or 15 minutes. It will take even longer to get back to studying if the messages are provoking or they are about things that the students are interested in. For example,

## If anybody tries...

Even though they missed out school study time,
or even though they lack the basic knowledge,
if they just learn the studying method suitable for them,
they can excel in their studies.

if they are exchanging text messages with their boyfriends or girlfriends, it will be very difficult for them to concentrate on the studies again.

Of course, there is difference between each individual, but I believe most of you have already experienced that your study is interrupted and your concentration is broken as a result of cell phones. So, it would be advisable that you remove the cell phone from your sight when you have to focus on your studies or work.

### Make an achievable weekly study plan

When you make a plan, you should not be too ambitious. With a plan for an excessive amount of studying, when things don't go as you planned, then it is likely that you won't be able to keep up with the studying materials that you have to finish, and eventually you will give up. If this kind of failure is repeated, you might develop a sense of defeat and you could think that you can't achieve anything. If you are behind the studying schedule, you have to re-plan it.

<u>Once you taste the joy of achieving a plan you made, you feel it is fun to study. You may now want to make a more extensive plan and feel the sense of greater achievement. In summation, you should make a plan within the boundary of your capabilities to achieve, and it is desirable for you to make</u>

<u>more detailed and specifically oriented plans.</u>

For example, you can make such plans as, 'Memorize 10 English words in 30 minutes' or 'Solve two pages of practical math problems in one hour'. Specific plans will give you stronger willpower to achieve them and increase your concentration, too. If you lack the concentration, it is advisable to make plans in short time periods, for example in one hour blocks.

If you have a plan, you won't face a situation where you sit at the desk but do not know at all what to do. It is not just about studying. Even for your work at your job, if you make it a habit to make plans, you are more likely to make greater achievements.

**Pray earnestly and follow the study plan**

It is more important to follow your plan than just to make it. In order to make sure you follow your plans, you can keep the record of what you study every day. If you write down whatever you study each day, you can check yourself as to whether you made the most of your time. Also, because you can check at a glance how much you have studied, you can feel the sense of achievement, too.

But above all, before you begin to study, pray for a little while with concentration. When you pray earnestly for 10 to

30 minutes, your thoughts and mind will be calm and steady, and then you will be able to focus on your studies. Now, you can just sit at the desk and begin to follow your study plan.

At first, you might be able to concentrate only for a short period of time. But the important thing is that you must never give up. Each day, no matter what you are doing, you have to stop whatever it is you are doing and go to study at the fixed time.

As you keep the promise with yourself day after day, then you can also control your mind. So, I hope you will try to keep the promise with yourself, even for small things. As you continue to control your mind and thoughts, it will be great power in you and you will be able to achieve great things.

### Driving away idle thoughts

But sometimes, even though you sit at the desk to keep up with your plan, you might not be able to concentrate because of idle thoughts. Then, why not try writing down the things that come into your mind? If you try not to have idle thoughts, they come into your mind more.

This is called, "rebound effect." Rather than trying to suppress your idle thoughts, if instead you express them by writing them down, they will go away to some extent.

If you cannot take untruthful thoughts off your mind,

just write them down on a piece of paper and put large 'X's on them. Then, you can pray about them during your prayer time. Pray that you will be able to drive away such thoughts. Then the Holy Spirit can help you get rid of the source of idle thoughts. This is the surest way to get rid of your idle thoughts.

You really need to try all your best to drive away idle thoughts and study with concentration. Just as you cannot wait for an apple to fall from the tree into your hands, you have to try hard to get rid of idle thoughts.

Sometimes it helps if you read out loud what you are reading. You won't have the leisure to have other thoughts because you focus on reading the book out loud. When God pours His grace and strength upon your effort and when the Holy Spirit helps you, you can have great power of concentration.

> In addition

# Addiction to TV and its withdrawal response

A college professor in the United States did research on people who watch TV excessively. He had the subjects put a beeper on them and he called them on the beeper 6-8 times a day. Whenever they received a call they were to write down what they were doing and their emotional state of the moment. This showed some interesting results.

In general, people think they can get rid of stress by watching TV. But according to the research, the more you watch TV, the joy you get from the TV decreases, but the nervousness you get after you turn off TV increases. In other words, when you watch TV more and more, you are not watching it because it is fun but just because you cannot turn it off.

Watching TV can become addictive. It is proved by the fact that it produces withdrawal effects. According to research conducted by a team at the University of Chicago, when they were not allowed to watch TV, those who seem to have addiction to TV were irritated, and they just wandered around in the living room, without being able to accomplish anything.

Furthermore, the contents on TV are becoming increasingly more violent and sensual. There are some study results that say such TV contents can increase anti-social behaviors as well.

## \<Dangers of TV addiction\>

### 1. Sleep and behavioral disorders

The more you watch TV, the more you distance yourself from activities like doing homework, exercising, or doing other hobbies. Watching TV doesn't require you of a high level of thinking skills, and thus it decreases your creativity. And watching TV can even cause sleep disorders and behavioral disorders.

### 2. Obesity

Many people have their meals or snacks while watching TV. It is difficult for the human brain to detect that you are already full if you are focused on the program contents on television, and it is likely that you will overeat, thereby increasing the chance of becoming obese.

### 3. Violence

There are some beneficial program contents on TV, but the majority of the programming contains harmful contents. While watching sensual or violent scenes you innately desire to follow such examples, or you become less careful and more receptive of such behaviors.

- Part 5 -

# A Guide for Better Grades

"...for it is sanctified
by means of the word of God and prayer."
-
1 Timothy 4:5

Many experts on education say that knowing how to study is more important than having high IQ. So, in order to get good grades you should find the effective methods to study and apply them to yourself. Nowadays, there are many kinds of self-help 'know-hows' and methods of studying that are recommended by the experts. But you should find the kind of studying methods that suits you the best.

Recently, people say 'self-guided studying' is important. Easily put, it means you have to study by yourself. Beginning with setting the goal of your studies, you have to do everything by yourself in choosing the materials and methods of studying, and evaluating the results of your studying. You might feel it is hard in the beginning. But in the long-run, the achievement level is much higher when you do everything by yourself.

Let's talk about some basic studying methods. You can apply them in your actual practice and make self-improvement strategies to bring up your grades.

## Secret 1: Enjoy your studying

People remember the things they are interested in very well. For example, some people know a lot about a particular sport such as the height, weight, position, and winning rate of a particular athlete in that sport. Or, some others like cars very much. They know the brand, year, engine performance and other special features of many cars.

Do they find it hard to memorize all those things? In most cases they don't. They have interest in the things they like, and they can easily input the information on such things. When you study, you can study better if you feel it is easy and fun. On the contrary, if you feel negatively, that it is hard, you cannot study so well. So, let me introduce a method with which you can study easily.

<u>How do you memorize the things that you have to memorize? Can you memorize well just by reading the books? No. Things that are dry and not interesting are not easily input into your memory. In such cases, you can utilize your feelings. If you have a strong feeling when you see or hear something, that memory lasts for a long time.</u>

Feelings make the knowledge go deep into the memory device. The stronger the feeling, the deeper the memory is planted. The feelings of untruth are the main cause of idle thoughts, but good feelings can help with your studying. If you utilize your feelings in memorizing things, you can more easily memorize dry and uninteresting things. We can understand this from the different ways of forming our memories.

### Use your feelings to memorize

There are four different types of memory formation. Different memories will last for different periods of time according to how you form your memory. (It is explained in more detail in the book *Spirit, Soul, and Body*.)

**The first type is just 'passing it by'.**

When you see or hear something, you don't pay attention and you just let it pass by. For instance, if you are daydreaming in class, later you won't remember anything you heard. Because you didn't pay attention at all to what the teacher was saying, it came in one ear and straight out the other ear. This kind of memory does not remain in your brain at all. The same goes for worship services. If you attend the service in spirit and truth you can remember the sermon, but if you have idle thoughts during the sermon you won't remember anything.

**The second type is 'casual association'.**

In the class, you listened to the teacher understanding what the teacher was saying. You think you know it for sure at the moment. But after several days, you cannot remember it any more. If you store things in a basket that has no lid, and if you shake the basket, the things will fall out. Likewise, what you casually stored in your brain can be easily displaced and forgotten.

**The third type is 'planting the memory firmly'.**

Before the class begins, the teacher says, "We will have a test at the end of the class. You will get one point deducted for each wrong answer you give." Then, the students will try to focus on the contents of the class. This is the process of 'planting'. If you pay extra attention to what you study, the memory lasts for a relatively longer period of time.

But there is another type of memory that lasts longer than others.

**It is the fourth type, which is 'to plant it in both the brain and heart'.**

This is to plant the information not just in the brain but also in the heart along with the impression and feelings associated with the information. For example, in the class a teacher you like very much asked you a question about

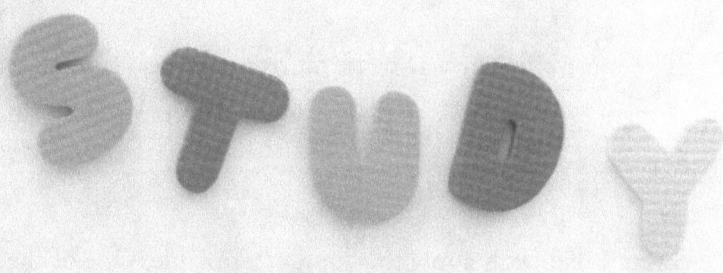

## Studying

Consider studying easy and fun.
The feelings of untruths are the main cause of idle thoughts.
Good feelings help with the studies.
For contents that do not have particular characteristics, you can relate them with something else to increase your feeling about it. Then, it will be planted both in the heart and memory and it will last longer.

the subject in the class. Fortunately you gave the correct answer because you went over the lesson beforehand, and the teacher commended you. You were really happy about it. You probably wouldn't forget about that question and answer situation. You did not only remember the answer to that question, but you also planted in your heart the joy of being commended at the moment you gave the correct answer.

The most efficient way to memorize what you studied is the fourth type, which is to plant memory both in your brain and heart.

Even unbelievers apply this kind of principle. One of the examples is to memorize with association. It is to familiarize with or have strong impression of things that are uninteresting and unimpressive by associating them with something else. You can associate them with objects or people, or you can amplify the feeling through the five senses, namely sound, color, smell, taste, and touch.

For example to memorize spelling "geography", make a sentence using the letters of the word to make a sentence like: "<u>G</u>eorge <u>E</u>llis's <u>o</u>ld <u>g</u>randmother <u>r</u>ode <u>a</u> <u>p</u>ig <u>h</u>ome <u>y</u>esterday. G-E-O-G-R-A-P-H-Y the first letter of each word of the sentence helps you remember the spelling.

But if you try to memorize every single thing using this

method, the associations themselves might make things complicated. Therefore, simple repetition might be more effective depending on the case.

It is also good method to chant something out loud or to put a melody on the contents that you want to memorize and sing it. In English, the Romance languages and German, young children learn to sing their ABC's. Also, we have a song in Korea with the names of the 66 books of the Bible so we can memorize them easily.

## How to improve the grades in the subjects you are not good at

There is one more way to enjoy your studies. It is to begin to like the subjects that you used to dislike.

If you just avoid or give up on a subject you dislike, you will only dislike it more and your grades will fall. Then, even if the grades of the subjects you like are very high, the average cannot go any higher. Therefore, you should begin to like the subjects that you dislike, so that you can do better in the subjects that you are not good at.

For example, do you hate math and find it very difficult? Why don't you overcome math just as Jacob wrestled with an angel and overcame. *You can change your feeling* thinking, "I do not dislike math. I have begun to like math now," and begin to overcome math.

For your information, experts say math grades are directly proportional to patience. If you wrestle with the math problems and solve them, your feelings will change. You can gain the confidence that you can also do it, and math will feel different to you. Here, what you have to remember is that you have to tackle the easy questions first. If you try to solve difficult problems from the beginning and fail, you might get adverse effects from it.

Those of you who dislike English can also try this method. There was a person who wanted to study English. He decided to invest half an hour every morning. For several days he was sticking to his plans, but on a certain day, he could not keep it because he was reading a newspaper and doing other things. And later he gave such excuses as he didn't have time to study.

When he analyzed his situation and why he couldn't study, he realized that he did not invest enough of duration of time to study, and it was also irregular. So he decided to study English the first thing in the morning and then read the newspapers, which he liked. As he kept on studying for at least half an hour a day, his proficiency in English improved, and his dislike towards English also disappeared.

<u>If you dislike English, you need to find the reason why you came to dislike it. Then, you can try to find the good points</u>

<u>of studying English and try to love it.</u>

In a sense, you can just 'play' with English. You can also reward yourself if you kept your promise to spend a certain amount of time in studying English. You can do a simple exercise to relax your body and mind, or refresh yourself listening to praise songs. You might eat something delicious for a change. If you reward and encourage yourself whenever you achieve your goals, you can feel the sense of accomplishment and increase your patience, too.

As you invest your time and effort, you would come to like the subjects in which you are not good or that you dislike. Gradually your grades in those subjects will go up, too. It's not only about studying. The same principle can be applied for anything you don't like. You can try to change your feeling of dislike into a good feeling.

People usually want to have what they like and avoid what they do not like. They try to keep a distance from those who have very different characters or who do not get along with them. They just want to be friends with those who are nice to them. Such people cannot become the kind of big vessel that God wants. They should be able to accept and embrace all kinds of people.

This principle can be applied to the personal religious life, too. If you do not like praying, you should not just think,

'Praying is difficult. I want to pray well like others, but I can't. Perhaps prayer is not my thing.' You have to change your thoughts into such thoughts as, 'Prayer is conversation with God. It's something fun. It's so good that I can receive answers to my prayers!' And make it a habit to pray for half an hour every day. As you pray day after day, you will feel the fun and know the sweet taste of prayer.

Therefore, we should love everything except untruth and evil. In apartments, when there is noise from the upstairs, like little kids running around or playing the piano, a person might wish that the family upstairs would move out. But even in this case, you can have positive thoughts like, 'They must be happy that they have lovely children! If I had children they'd be running around, too!' Then, you will not have any uncomfortable feelings.

## Secret 2: Do the previews and reviews

If you do the previews and reviews, you can hold on to the things that can easily slip away. You can also plant what you stored in memory deep in your heart. To the extent that we see or hear about an object repeatedly, our brains will remember it more deeply. If you do the previews and reviews before and after the class, it means you learn the lesson three times. Of course, everyone knows it is important to do the

## Try to love!

If you just distance yourself from
or give up something you don't like,
you will only dislike it more.
It will be your weak point permanently.
You have to find the good points from it
and try to love it.

previews and reviews of classes. But there are not many students who actually do it.

There is a lawyer who passed the bar exam, Higher Civil Service Exam, and the Foreign Affairs Service Exam during the three years of his college life. He says the secret was the 'review'. Those who failed the exams did not even read the books three times, but he read them five to ten times. You might become apprehensive thinking 'how can I find the time to read such thick books', but if you actually try it, it is not as difficult as you initially thought.

Of course, books about law and public administration are thick and they have specialized vocabulary. So, initially, you might have to spend a significant amount of time to finish the book. But the second time would be much easier. And it will be even easier the third time. As the number of times you read the book increases, the time needed to read the book decreases, and it becomes much easier to finish the book.

Now let us think of specific ways to do the previews and reviews.

The previews can have tremendous effect on the class. If you learn most of the things that will be covered in the class, you might be bored during the actual class. So, you should just skim through the contents that will be covered in the class so you can develop curiosity about the subject and focus on the class. It is best to do the preview the day before the class or right before the class. During the actual preview, you can go through the titles and subtitles to learn the flow and then do a quick skimming of the main contents, and mark the parts that are difficult.

There is huge difference between the students who did a preview of the class and those students who learned the lesson for the first time. The former would have more focus and interest in the subject, and it's much easier for them to remember what is covered in the class.

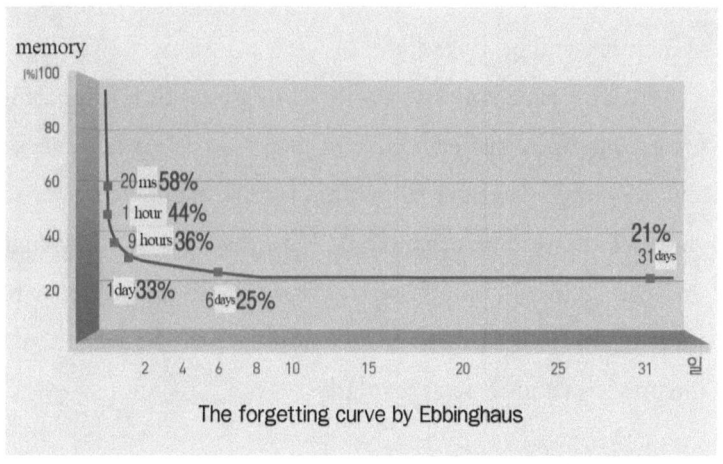
The forgetting curve by Ebbinghaus

After the class is over, it is a very good habit to do a quick review of the class, rather than just closing the book right away. If the situation doesn't allow, you should do a review before you go to bed that day.

According to the research of the psychologist, Hermann Ebbinghaus, people forget half of what they memorized after an hour, 70% after a day, and 80% after a month. So, even though you have memorized something thoroughly, you should review within an hour or at least within a day, so the rate of forgetting will decrease dramatically.

Therefore, you should develop the habit of reviewing all your classes each day. You should not just review each day's classes, but you have to repeat them again and again until the contents are deeply planted in your heart. Reviewing is like locking the door of memory so that whatever was input cannot escape. The more you repeat, the more firmly the door of memory will be locked.

If you do your previews and reviews all the time, preparing for exams becomes easy. If you don't do any previews or reviews and if you have to prepare for the exam, you have to study a large volume of material. Also, the kind of knowledge that you cram will be very quickly forgotten. You will have to study again later. Therefore, you should develop a habit to do the previews and reviews regularly.

## Previews and reviews will help you improve your grades.

If you only try to study right before the exams,
the volume will be enormous.
Also, the kind of knowledge you cram overnight will be forgotten easily and you will have to study them later again.

There is a student whose grades increased from the 50$^{th}$ to the 1$^{st}$ in his class. His secret was to thoroughly read each textbook of all the subjects ten times. The first time is always the most difficult. In fact, it is not easy to read the textbooks of all the subjects ten times. But he read all the letters in the textbooks when he read them for the first time. And to make it easier it is important to pay attention in the class.

After reading the textbook once thoroughly, he had many questions. Here, he acquired the answers through other books, from teachers, or on the Internet, and noted down all the related information in the respective textbooks. Once this process was done, he had the custom-made best textbook for him alone. From this moment he began reading the book ten times. When he finished this process and read the textbook, he could feel it so much easier to read it.

After reading the textbook five to seven times, you'd understand the relations among different chapters as a whole. Furthermore, you'd also be able to see which part is more important, and you'd even be able to make a test or exam for yourself. From the 8$^{th}$ to the 10$^{th}$ time is the process to reaffirm the memory. If you take a test after reading the textbook ten times, you'd feel like you are taking an open-book test.

Doing previews and reviews is very useful when you learn the words of God, too. Before the worship service, you read the reading passage of the sermon. In case of a series of sermons or lectures on a particular book of the Bible, you can review the previous week's sermon. And now, you can worship in spirit and truth. After the worship service, you try to remember the message you heard and put it in your heart. If you are so busy the whole day that there's no time, then you can meditate on the message you heard before you go to bed.

If you are greatly touched by the message or if you realize something within yourself through the sermon, you can input the message even better. And if you cultivate in your heart what you've realized, then that word of God will completely become yours. On the other hand, however, if you just hear and forget the message, it is of no use to hear the word thousands of times.

You should review the message, and it is better to listen to it again during that week. If you read the summary after a week, it will remain in your memory for a longer time. If you continuously keep the word of God in your mind week after week, you will have richness of the word of God in you. In case of pastors or workers, if you are asked to deliver a message impromptu, you can do it by the help and inspiration of the Holy Spirit.

The same goes for memorizing Bible verses. You can

memorize one verse a day, and you have to memorize them again later because you will forget them as time goes. Perhaps you can review all the verses you have memorized once a week.

## Secret 3: Good life habits

In order to excel academically, you should manage your personal life, too. You have to manage your fitness, time, and habits to increase the effectiveness of your studying.

**For example, to study well, you should get an adequate amount of sleep.**

It is said that some old scholars poked themselves with needles when they got sleepy studying late at night. But rather than overworking like this, it is more effective to get enough rest and study with a clear mind. Your brain function will deteriorate if you lack sleep. Your understanding and memory power will fall. If you study when you are tired, you will soon become exhausted.

On the contrary, if you get enough sleep and study when your brain is functioning well, you can digest a greater amount in a shorter time period. Those who are taking the college entrance exam must feel impatient and pressed for the moment. But you have to sleep at least five to six hours a day. Of course, if your fitness and health is really good, you can sleep a little less. The important thing is you should understand your bio-rhythm and get enough sleep.

**It is also important to have a regular, well-balanced diet.**
Some students skip meals to sleep more or often eat fast foods to save time. But this kind of diet can make your body sick or weak, so you should be careful. It could be a rather negative point to your studying.

You also need to control the amount of food you eat. Especially, right before you study, you should stop when you feel like, "I want just a little more." If you overeat, you get drowsy and your concentration will decrease. It is not good to eat too little either. If you are still hungry, you might have idle thoughts.

Other than these, when you come back home from outside, you should wash yourself and clean up your surroundings. Your mind will be at comfort when your appearance and surroundings are clean and squared away. If you live a life that gives out the aroma of the Lord, self-management will be done automatically. If you are an imitator of the Lord and resemble Him, you will also be like Him in your appearance, attitude, and behavior.

The most important thing, of course, is your will to get good grades. You should have a dream to give glory to God through academic excellence and the will-power to achieve it. When you accomplish what you have decided, your will-power will become stronger. In order to achieve strong will-power, you have to train yourself to do what you have decided from small things.

> In addition

# 21-day project for 'habit of success'

John Maxwell, who has written many books, primarily focusing on leadership, said, "Success comes in taking many small steps." And "Success is achieved in inches, not miles." Our little life habits that we carry on daily will probably decide our success.

Even the Great Wall or the Pyramids began from one piece of stone, and the Grand Canyon began from a little winding of the stream. Little habits can make a great difference in achieving our success. Successful people continue to do the things that unsuccessful people do only from time to time.

Some neuro-linguistic programming scientists say it takes about 21 days for a certain action to become a habit. Our brain will reject something for which synapse has not been formed by enough repetition.

Whether it is to wake up early in the morning, to read books, reduce TV watching, or controlling the diet, we have to consciously try at least for 21 days until that action settles in the body.

It's because it takes at least 21 days for our bio-clock to be readjusted. After 21 days, you can carry on that particular action without having to try consciously. This is called the 'Twenty-one Day Law'.

**<Making a good habit>**

Plan ⇒ Do ⇒ See!!

1. Write down the habits you'd like to make/change
2. Focus on one thing to carry it out.
3. Reward yourself when you carried it out, and make a standard of self-punishment for not carrying it out.
4. Promise the people around you that you will keep your plan.
5. Make a checklist to check whether you are carrying out the particular action for 21 days.
6. Do an overall evaluation with your family once a week.
7. If successful, you can move on to another kind of habit.

How about increasing your strength to change your habits with the help of God as Daniel received the answer to his prayer after praying for 21 days?

- Part 6 -

# Studying with Heart

"The LORD will make you the head
and not the tail,
and you only will be above,
and you will not be underneath,
if you listen to the commandments
of the LORD your God,
which I charge you today,
to observe them carefully,"

-

Deuteronomy 28:13

IQ is not the only thing that accounts for academic excellence and success in life. In order to be a successful person, one has to be equipped with various characters such as those expressed in the EQ(Emotional Quotient) and the SQ(Social Quotient). Recently, they have developed such concepts as CQ(Cultural Quotient), and AQ(Adversity Quotient). We can increase such capabilities if we lead a good religious life.

If you cultivate your heart to be good soil by leading a good life as a believer, you can focus on your studies without having idle thoughts even though you do not have high intelligence or even though your circumstances are not favorable. The key principle in studying is to study with the heart rather than only with the brain. Put more simply, it means your heart takes control over your studying. Here, the heart refers to the heart that is cultivated to be good soil. Now, what kind of heart is a heart of good soil?

## Heart of good soil

Good soil is the best soil for plants to grow and for each seed to bear the most possible fruit. In the same way, a person with the heart of good soil would attentively listen to the word of God and obey it as it is, thereby receiving answers to prayers and blessings.

This heart of good soil has not been calloused but is soft. It means it is very receptive of God's words. They believe and practice His words as it is. Good soil does not have rocks in it, so the seed of the Word can take root deeply. Because they don't love the world, they do not hesitate as to whether or not to obey the Word. Thus, they don't have struggle within themselves. Because they don't have the untruths in them, it is not difficult for them to practice the Word.

Furthermore, because they don't have any forms of evil, they wouldn't have any idle thoughts or fleshly thoughts. They can discern the will of God correctly and hear the voice of the Holy Spirit clearly, so they can make the most of their abilities.

We can subdue our circumstances and control our mind to the extent that we cultivate our heart to be good soil through the word of God. Proverbs 4:23 says, *"Watch over your heart with all diligence, for from it flow the springs of life."* It is very important to control our mind. We cannot say we have subdued our own heart as long as we have untruths in our heart. It's because even a little bit of untruth remaining could change and corrupt our heart.

Understanding this, we should quickly remove spiritual rocks from our heart and uproot all the thorn bushes. Namely, when we cast off all the untruths that make us disobey the words of God, we will have a heart of good soil. We will then be able to control our mind, too. Why is it that we can excel academically when we cultivate a heart of good soil?

## Seeing with eyes of faith in everything

There are some students who do not have the will to study because they have negative and passive attitudes. They only think, "It's useless to study. I am not smart enough to get good grades." On the contrary those who have the heart of good soil have a positive and active attitude when they study. With faith they say, "I can do it with the strength of the Lord. I can give glory to God and achieve my dream by studying hard." Joshua and Caleb are very good examples.

It was at the time when the sons of Israel reached Canaan after the Exodus. They selected an elder from each of the twelve tribes to spy on the land. When the spies went and saw the land, the people there were big and strong. They became disheartened.

Only Joshua and Caleb professed boldly, "They are our prey." It was not some groundless claim. It was profession of faith and hope and confidence. They said, *"If the LORD is pleased with us, then He will bring us into this land and give it to us – a land which flows with milk and honey"* (Numbers 14:8-9).

<u>The task of studying for students may be as difficult as the task of conquering the Canaan Land for the sons of Israel. However, if they have faith, they can conquer it saying, "They are our prey."</u>

There was a teenage boy who wanted to become an excellent lawyer. Studying law is not something that's easy. However, he had had many conversations with his mother about his faith, dreams, and visions from early childhood, and he had the faith that he could do anything in the Lord. He tried to improve his shortcomings while listening to the sermons. He always relied on God and asked God to give him the wisdom to excel academically.

He also listened to his mother's advice that it is important to carry out whatever he decided to do and to keep on studying hard to achieve his goal. As a result, he received the President's Award for Educational Excellence and graduated from high school with honors. Eventually he went to one of the most prestigious law schools in the United States. He was getting closer to achieving his dream to be a lawyer.

Hebrews 11:1 says, *"Now faith is the assurance of things hoped for..."* Even though we cannot see the substance of something now with physical eyes, eventually what we hope for with faith will come true. What are you looking forward to? We have to see everything with the eyes of faith whether it is studying or work. Those who have the heart of good soil will keep the truth having the eyes of faith, and they will receive what they have believed they would.

## Do not stop until the goal is achieved

When you set a goal to cover a certain volume of study materials for the day, you might face some temptations. You might want to sleep because you feel very tired or you might want to go out and have fun. Your friends might ask you to hang out with them today and study tomorrow.

In these situations, those who have good heart soil will not either give in or think, 'I'll study hard starting tomorrow.' They will achieve their goal for the day no matter what. They will not succumb to any temptation or any hardship.

<u>Those who have good heart soil do not get shaken when they face difficulties in their circumstances, trouble with</u>

other people, or other types of failures. It's because they have a strong factor of EQ, the power of the emotional quotient.

They control their feelings in any kind of hardship and overcome those difficulties. They do not lose heart. They do not get disheartened or give up, but keep on going towards the goal. The apostle Paul inspired countless Christians throughout the generations.

He said in Philippians 3:13-14, *"Brethren, I do not regard myself as having laid hold of it yet; but one thing I do forgetting what lies behind and reaching forward to what lies ahead, I press on toward the goal for the prize of the upward call of God in Christ Jesus."* Let us think about his life based on the five criteria of EQ.

**The ability to recognize personal emotions, value them and accept them**

Some say that they do whatever they feel like doing. But those who have heart of good soil do not really need to understand their own feelings. It's because they always have the best feeling. Their emotions are non-fluctuating and they don't become confused concerning their personal emotions.

Because they have no envy, jealousy, hatred, or anger they do not become bewildered wondering why they have certain emotions. Neither do they become nervous thinking they

## Heart of good-soil

Those who have hearts of good-soil
do not have any evil or untruths in them,
so they can focus on their studies.
They study faithfully as their heart guides
them. In this way they can achieve the best
possible results.

shouldn't have certain emotions.

Of course, we sometimes have spiritual mourning for the kingdom of God and for other souls, but it is different from being gloomy or bewildered.

Paul was always rejoicing although he was living a challenging life for the spreading of the gospel. He said in Philippians 4:4, *"Rejoice in the Lord always; again I will say, rejoice!"* It was to comfort the believers. 2 Corinthians 13:11 says, *"Finally, brethren, rejoice, be made complete, be comforted, be like-minded, live in peace; and the God of love and peace will be with you."* He could comfort the believers because his mind always had joy and peace.

### The ability to control personal impulses and emotions such as nervousness and anger

Your evil will be removed to the extent that you cultivate the heart of good soil, and you will not have such emotions as nervousness or anger to that same extent. You can control your desires, too, and your mind will always be as calm as a smooth lake.

The apostle Paul had been in many stressful situations. His life was threatened many times while spreading the gospel. He had been wrongfully beaten or imprisoned. An ordinary person would have got a disease or even died of stress. But Paul's heart was always filled with joy. He praised God even when he was severely beaten and put into jail.

### The ability to encourage oneself, even in failure, without getting disheartened

Not becoming disheartened is one of the most evident attributes of the heart of good soil. Even after failures, those with good heart soil rejoice and give thanks with their faith in God. Paul had had a great number of frustrating situations. There were persecutions and distress awaiting him in the fields of preaching the gospel.

Acts 14:19-20 says, *"But Jews came from Antioch and Iconium, and having won over the crowds, they stoned Paul and dragged him out of the city, supposing him to be dead. But while the disciples stood around him, he got up and entered the city. The next day he went away with Barnabas to Derbe."* He was beaten and practically dead when they threw his body out of the city.

But he stood back up again like a tumbling doll and continued to preach the gospel. He said that despite the series of ordeals, *"we are afflicted in every way, but not crushed; perplexed, but not despairing"* (2 Corinthians 4:8), and *"But in all these things we overwhelmingly conquer through Him who loved us"* (Romans 8:37).

When you study or initiate something for the glory of God, you might face a failure. Or it may look like you failed.

Nevertheless, those who have love for God and hope of Heaven like those that the apostle Paul had, they can become more than just conquerors. Even if they fail, if they stand back up and look up to God again, God works for the good of everything.

### The ability to empathize with other people's feelings

Those who have the heart of good-soil have the ability to empathize with others' feelings, and they understand others' behavior. They consider others first and seek the benefit of others over their own. In doing so, there will be no animosity; there will be nobody that can't be understood and no hatred. This becomes their power.

For the sake of the Lord and saving the souls, the apostle Paul did not take the things that he could have enjoyed. Some believers asked him if it was OK for them to eat meat that was offered as sacrifice to idols. Paul himself could eat it with faith, but in consideration of those who had weak faith, he said he would not eat meat forever if it could make the brothers stumble.

### Social ability to cooperate with other people

Those who have the heart of good soil will have harmony in a group and pursue peace with everybody. Even when there is conflict, they become mediators and peacemakers. They are on good terms with school friends or co-workers.

Paul understood better than any others how important peace is in every matter. Though he was under so much persecution, he never retaliated with evil. He said in Hebrews 12:14, *"Pursue peace with all men, and the sanctification without which no one will see the Lord."* He emphasized that having peace is an attribute that the believers must have in order to be able to see the Lord.

Students who often quarrel with others and complain cannot focus on their studies because their minds are not at peace. The same goes for company employees. If they have trouble with others every time they do something, they will lose their concentration and efficiency in their work. Even if they have great knowledge and skills, as long as they do not have peace it's difficult for them to make the best of what they have. It's because there is no work that can be accomplished without the cooperation of other co-workers.

So, the ability to pacify is necessary not only when you study but also when you utilize your knowledge that you have already acquired. Having a vast range of knowledge will be useless if you cannot utilize it. The ability to utilize your knowledge is wisdom, and wisdom is more important thing. The great wisdom given by God comes down upon the heart that is pure and that pursues peace (James 3:17).

As mentioned above, if you have the heart of good-soil,

you will not change your mind or give up until you achieve your goal. You can control your thoughts and emotions, and thus, you can concentrate on your studies or work regardless of circumstances or external conditions.

This kind of persistence, with which we don't give up even in temptations or distress, is necessary in all areas of our lives. If we cultivate the heart of good-soil, we can have the highest marks in all areas of EQ and excel in our studies.

## You can do more than with your own capabilities

Most of Jesus' disciples were fishermen who did not have much education. Yet, they became apostles and taught so many people. They preached the gospel in front of the high priests, elders, and officials who had studied the Bible thoroughly.

Acts 4:13 says, *"Now as they observed the confidence of Peter and John and understood that they were uneducated and untrained men, they were amazed, and began to recognize them as having been with Jesus."* This was made possible by the help of the Holy Spirit. Jesus' disciples acquired a vast amount of spiritual knowledge from Jesus. After the Holy Spirit came, they understood that knowledge by heart. Anybody can do more than what they can do by their own ability if they receive the help of the Holy Spirit.

For example, if you lack power to memorize, you can cultivate a heart of good-soil. Then, you will be able to keep things in mind and remember well. If you engrave something that you have to remember in the heart, the Holy Spirit will remind you of it when necessary.

Before I accepted the Lord and when I was a student, I had taken many stimulant drugs called 'pep pills' to stay awake at night. This caused memory loss. To make things worse, I had to take many strong medicines while I had many sicknesses for seven years, and this caused even greater memory loss. But after all my diseases were healed by the power of God, it became different. Though I cannot remember all the details of events in distant past, God reminds me of the things that are necessary for sermons or counseling.

I have many schedules to follow in my ministry, but I do not make any notes. It's because the Holy Spirit reminds me of the things that I have to do at each moment. If I make an appointment with somebody, the Holy Spirit reminds me of it when the date is approaching.

In the theological college, once I got very good grades by the help of God and not by relying on my own memory power. It was when I was in the first year of theological college. Unfortunately I had final exams during my vowed prayer. But I couldn't change what I had vowed before God, and I just kept my vow. Then I had an amazing experience. I prayed briefly about the exam after I finished my vowed prayers each night, and God let me know the questions for the exam.

Those questions were on the actual exam, and I could finish both the vowed prayer and the final exam. When I prayed to God with genuine desire to give glory to God and not for my personal gain, God gave me limitless and mysterious power. It's not only about memory power but also power of understanding, too. We can understand even difficult contents with the help of the Holy Spirit. We can also learn good methods of studying.

Of course, after building up trust with God, His help can come upon us when we ask with faith. I hope you will be God's children who are trusted by Him so that you can receive the help of the Holy Spirit and achieve more than what you can achieve with your own ability.

Have a great dream to study hard and give glory to God. Cultivate your heart as good-soil and study faithfully. God will give you passion and wisdom and let you give glory to Him in your schools, families, workplaces, and business places. He will use you as noble instruments to save many souls.

> In addition

# Self-directed learning

There was a student who was lost because he did not have a dream. He was admitted to a college, but he chose his major without thinking about his career path. He thought he couldn't go on studying and told his parents he wanted to quit. This caused great conflict with his parents. The parents asked him which subject he was good at back in high school.

He remembered that he was talented in music and decided to major in voice. During one of his voice lessons, the teacher said, "I think conducting would be better for you, considering your personality." That changed his career path. He really liked conducting and had more fun studying about it. He wanted to study more and went to a graduate school.

There are surprisingly many students who do not know what to do with their futures. Some students are forced to study by their parents. Unless somebody makes a study plan for them, they find it hard to learn anything on their own. Self-directed learning cannot be achieved in a short period of time. They have to gain the know-how after making the plans and adjusting them many times by themselves.

### 1. Consider your aptitude

You have to objectively think about what you are talented at and what you like. If you can't figure it out yourself, you can consult your parents, counseling teachers, or professional organizations.

### 2. Set a goal

A clear goal has great effect on the grades, too. If the children are very young, their dreams may change every day, but the parents can still watch for and figure out what their children are good at and what fields they are interested in. Then, they should guide their children to set a goal which is consistent with the talents and aptitude of the children. Then, even though they do not tell their children to study all the time, they will find a way to study by themselves.

### 3. Make it a habit to read books

Reading improves the ability to understand the written contents and understand the intention of the writer. If they lack this kind of ability, they will find it hard to achieve self-directed learning even though they have desire to study and they can manage their time very well. Guiding little children to read a lot will help their self-directed learning.

- Part 7 -

# Real-life Keys to Studying Well

# Writing Skills Can Serve as the Fundamental for College Entrance

### Deaconess Heun Kim

Master's in Literature, Education Major, Ewah Woman's University
Researcher in Korea Vocational Ability Development Institute

Heun Kim says she had more fun in both her studies and religious life while doing her graduate studies and listening to the messages of Rev. Jaerock Lee. She earned scholarships for academic excellence earning straight A's during her Master's courses. She won the Grand Prize in the Book Review Contest for '*My Life My Faith*' that was held by *Christian Press* in September 2008. She says she understands the troubles that students might face and she wants to give them hope and help them set their career paths. Recently she acquired the certificate for Guide of Self-directed Learning.

## Q. What Can Be Done to Improve Writing Skills?

In today's education world, a great deal of emphasis is put on 'thinking power' and 'self-directed learning'. To improve thinking power and have the habit of self-directed learning, experts in education emphasize 'debate' and 'writing'.

The writing skills that the colleges require of the students are not just laying out words. Just filling your essay with 'good sentences' or just laying out the information that you have cannot score high points.

The colleges do not evaluate students' writing skills in itself, but tend to measure overall thinking power as to how they understand and logically analyze the problems at hand.

### Reading

'Reading' always comes together with 'writing' like a needle and thread. Most good writers read a lot, too. But just reading a lot and writing many reviews do not automatically expand your thinking power or improve your writing skills.

The first thing you have to do is to make a habit of enjoying reading. For example, you can begin reading books about a topic in which you are interested and then expand to other areas that are related to the topic. If a child wants to become a medical doctor, he/she can begin reading autobiographies of famous medical doctors, or he/she could read books about human anatomy.

Here, the parents can help their children choose the books with a broader view. For example, in order to become a good doctor, they need to be interested in people, and for this they could read books about psychology or morality. You can expand the area of your reading in this way.

### Conversation

After the reading, you need to talk about it with your parents or friends, even if it is a short conversation. Through the conversation, you can not only summarize your thoughts but also expand the scope of your thinking by listening to other people's opinions. But it might be difficult to allot particular time slot for this type of conversation.

Depending on home dining etiquette or rules, it may be quite natural to talk about the book you've read at the dinner table. You can talk about it during a walk, too. Also, after the worship service, parents can talk about the sermon with their children so they can summarize the sermon and which parts of the sermon touched them. This may well help them improve their writing skills.

### Getting Your Writing Organized

In order to improve your writing, it's a good idea to read a lot or summarize the sermons and write the summary down. You don't have to stick to the formal style of introduction, body, and conclusion right from the beginning.

You can start by just stating an overview of the introduction, the main body, and the conclusion. Focus on the part that was the most interesting or most touching.

This is because you need to be able to put your own thoughts and feelings in your writing. This type of writing will help in your essay writing or making your portfolio for college entrance.

Here, the reason why you just jot down an overview is so that you can see the general contents at a glance. If you find it difficult to summarize in writing, it's OK to just write down anything that comes to your thoughts.

This is a kind of 'brainstorming'. Whether they are complete sentences or words, you can just write them down first and then put the pieces together like a puzzle later.

If you keep on summarizing three to four sermons each week over a period of time, you will gain confidence and ability in writing.

In summarizing sermons or writing a book review, if you do it with handwriting and not with a computer, it is better to use separate sheets of paper and bind them together rather than using a single notebook. This way, you can make use of the sheets freely, depending on how you categorize them.

Also, you can make annotations in the book itself. You can make notations on the blank pages referencing pages and dates or similarly annotating in the blank space in the book's margin. When you read the book next time, you will be reminded of the feelings that you had in reading the book. You can also expand the scope of your thoughts with those annotations when you read it once again or twice.

For exams that include essay writing, it is better to make a habit of writing in your own handwriting. It's simply because that's what you are going to have to do for the exam. If you do not practice writing in your hand, sometimes you might not be able to put together the thoughts in your head and write them down on the exam paper.

In order for you to write a logical essay within the given amount of time, you have to make the overview. By making the overview, you can stick to the logical flow and have a balance in the writing. Also, you can avoid meaningless repetitions or omitting something important. When you make an overview, first, you can put down the subject and write some simple words or sentences that will be part of the flow from introduction, to the main body, and to the conclusion. Also, you might even use a diagram or a table.

Such practices will help you greatly in the actual essay writing. You should understand what the examiner wants to see precisely. Write down the subject and overview on the question paper, and then give your answer on the answer sheet. This way you will be able to avoid digression and also manage the time well, too. Any examiner can easily tell if you have written the overview or not before writing the essay. If your essay is based on a good overview, usually you will be able to get a good score.

## Notes

Making scrap sheets of news articles or making notes about the articles can help you in your writing. Nowadays, you can make notes or memos on your smart-phones, and you can make a memo whenever you have an idea or leave quote from an article that you come across in the media.

When you take notes, it shouldn't be just the summary but you should also write down your thoughts about the content. You should also categorize your notes so you will be able to use them whenever you need them at a later time.

In my case, I assigned different colors to note different content types. I used yellow for sermons, blue for news articles, and green for any idea that suddenly pops up in my head. Also, you can categorize them by the topic, like a diary, or you can put them in a spreadsheet program in a computer to sort them systematically.

These kinds of habits will expand your knowledge and it will enable you to write about various subjects. Also, such notes and memos can help you when you create your portfolio, which is very important in college entrance and job search.

### Writing classes

If you want to learn professional writing, rather than just cramming what you have to do in writing, you might want to consider special classes or writing camps. There are some programs that can trigger the interest of the students and give them a taste of professional writing. Some examples are reading programs held by libraries or student reporter camps held by some newspaper companies.

It is not recommended that you learn just the writing skills that will let you pass the college entrance exams.

If you learn writing skills in your everyday life from childhood, it will give you the basic abilities to study and research in different subjects. It will eventually help you get better grades in particular subjects.

Analyzing the structure of the sentences, finding the main idea, and understanding the composition of the paragraphs in particular, can help you improve your language skills, even for foreign languages. Writing can give a boost to your studying ability because it improves both your power to think and your self-directed learning skills. All these eventually add up to give you greater proficiency and efficiency in studying.

Good writing skills accompany logical reasoning in

thinking, deductive thought, and ability to complete complex associations and organization. Thus it cannot be achieved in a short period of time. Therefore, students are encouraged to develop an interest in writing skills from childhood. I hope you will not just be ready for college entrance but become a competent individual in this twenty-first century through writing in everyday life.

### What is portfolio?

A portfolio is actually a large, flat, thin case for carrying loose papers or drawings or maps. But it also refers to a series of documents and certificates that can show the career knowledge, skills and special abilities that you possess.

The word portfolio is used in other areas, too, especially in finance, construction, or even fine art.

# There Are a Myriad of Reasons to Study...

**Deacon Hoyeon Kim**

Bachelor of Engineering at POSTECH, Master of Engineering at Seoul National University
Currently working at Samsung Electronics

Deacon Hoyeon Kim says he was very surprised after hearing the messages of Rev. Jaerock Lee of Manmin Central Church when he was in the 10th grade. He was just amazed that there was a church where God's miraculous works were actually taking place.

Since childhood, he admired those who were with Jesus, but being in the church, he felt like he was one of them. He was so thankful for the grace of God that guided him to come to this kind of church that was ministered by such a wonderful pastor. Though he was a student, he tried to find ways to pay back the grace of God.

Q. Was there any turning-point that made you decide to really study?

While I was praying to pay back the grace of God, I realized studying is one of the best things I could do, and I wanted to give glory to God by studying hard.

I thought if I could become the chancellor of Seoul National University, which is supposedly the best university in South Korea, I would be able to educate many students with the words of God, who would become influential people and leaders of the society. In that way the whole country could be changed as well. This hope became driving power that made me study hard.

Q. What was your childhood dream, and how are you working toward it now?

I loved Scientific Fiction cartoons and I wanted to become a scientist. I was especially interested in robotics. I wanted to study in the field of materials science and engineering, which is a study of basic materials. So, I applied for the Materials Science and Engineering major of POSTECH, Pohang

University of Science and Technology.

Then I got my Master's degree in Materials Science and Engineering in the graduate school of Seoul National University. During the graduate course, I was selected as a researcher who could do science research instead of the mandatory military service, and I began to work at the R&D center of Hyosung business group. Now, I am working as a researcher developing 'next generation' products.

Q. How did you study to achieve your dream?

First of all, I began by eliminating the things that could disturb my studying. Namely, I quit comic books and TV. I read the comic books and watched TV thinking that it would relieve my stress, but it was only momentary. Later, the contents from it that remained in my memory disturbed my studying. At last I did away with those things. It was not that I tried to quit even though I wanted to read comic books and watch TV so much, but I was able to quit easily having the God-given hope and thinking about the benefits I would get after quitting.

Next, I focused in the classes the best I could. I also did

previews and reviews of the classes daily. In less than a month I could see the effects. I was barely in top 10 of my class but I went up to the first in class. I was also able to maintain that position until graduation from high school.

Q. How did you overcome difficulties while you were studying?

I think it's a natural course of things to have some ups and downs when you study. The important thing is how you overcome hardships. In my case, I encouraged myself thinking about the love of God, of the Lord, and of my parents.

I thought about God who was guiding me. I was encouraged when I was looking forward to the day I could give God joy through my efforts. I always tried to remember that it is a duty of a student to study hard and also a way to store up rewards in Heaven.

Q. How did you manage your grades?

Even in my senior year of high school, I slept at least six hours a day and I spent the whole day at the church every

Sunday. Nevertheless, I could still get good grades, and I had some secrets.

Above all, I focused on the classes. If you do not learn the materials covered in the class itself, you have to spend a lot more time to learn it later. Therefore, whatever was covered in the class, I understood it and memorized it in the class. It was possible because I did the previews and reviews.

When I didn't have enough time, I just skimmed through what was going to be covered in the class for 5 or 10 minutes right before the class. The magnitude of understanding the class is completely different just by doing that. And after the class was over, I read the notes I made during the class and remembered the contents covered.

As I kept on doing this, I didn't have to study so much for final exams. I could still get good grades just by going over the contents that I understood each day.

In my studying time, I reviewed the problems or contents I could not fully understand in each day's class. For the subjects that needed constant work (Math, English, and Korean), I studied a certain volume every day and tried to improve my understanding and application.

In the buses going to church or going home, I remembered what I studied for the second time with my eyes closed. Then, my body could relax while learning what I studied by heart.

I simplified my life pattern, too. I just went to the school, home, and church, in order to avoid any waste of time. I also prayed fervently almost every day at a designated time of the day. It was like a refreshment period that made the tiredness go away. I received new strength every day.

## Q. How can one get better grades in high school?

Studying is much like building a tower. Without the knowledge of middle school courses, you cannot get good grades in high school. So, if you do not have the proper basic knowledge of middle school courses, you have to study them again. There is no short-cut to studying. In case of mathematics which many students find difficult, all the courses from the first year of middle school and to the last year of high school are inter-connected with one another.

But it does not mean it is too late for high school students.

There is a way. Even if they don't understand everything, they should still pay close attention in class and do the previews(5-10 minutes) and reviews(within an hour after class). Then, they can study the middle school courses during the vacations.

You might wonder when you'd be able to finish all the courses, but when high school students study middle school materials, it is usually very easy and they can finish them quickly. Then, while they are studying middle school courses they will begin to understand contents of the high school classes that they didn't understand initially, and they will begin to feel more interested in their studies.

It'd be easier for them to study the subjects that involve memorizing. In order to memorize well, you shouldn't just try to cram, but you need to understand the contents. It's not fun at all to try to memorize without understanding the subject. The memory span is reduced and retention doesn't last long either.

The best way to understand the subject is to pay attention in the class. Then, you won't have to allocate so much time to memorize the contents again. Preparing for the exam, you will be reminded of what you heard in the class while you read the textbook material once or twice again.

### Q. Any advice for students now?

Religious life and studying are not separate from each other. When we begin to rely on God from the smaller things keeping God-given hope for the future, He will guide us in the prosperous way. There are a myriad of reasons why a student has to study.

Also, it is not something difficult to get good grades. As you try to change yourself based on what you realized through the sermons each week, you will get the peace and joy coming from above, and this will give you strength to study better.

I hope you will overcome the pressure of exams and the burdensome feeling about college entrance with faith in God, and become individuals of excellence in both your Christian lives and in this world as well.

# Try Your Best Having Faith and Confidence

Brother Suk June Moon

Graduated from International School of Qingdao
Studying at Yonsei University

Suk June has gone to school in the United States and in China because of his father's job locations. He studies hard with a positive mindset and with a good dream in the Lord. He received the President's Award for Academic Excellence both in 2009 and 2010, maintaining a GPA of 4.0 out of 4.0.

Q. How did you come to study in the United States?

I went to Oregon in 2006 because my father got a job

there. I was in 4$^{th}$ grade when I went to the United States, and everything was unfamiliar. I was nervous that I had to live in a country where the language, culture, customs, and appearances are different.

At first, I could only say very basic things like "Where is the restroom?" in English. But I began to learn the language little by little with a positive mindset based on faith in God. People were surprised that I learned English very quickly.

I went to Sexton Mountain Elementary School, and I couldn't speak at all in the class. When classmates talked to me, I didn't understand what they were saying, and I'd reply something completely irrelevant. They laughed at me, but I wasn't ashamed or discouraged. I just believed that I'd do fine.

I tried my best in math because it was the only subject I could do better than the other classmates. Then, I began to excel in other subjects one by one. I could speak English with greater fluency after about a year and a half. I took part in the school activities, too.

I ran for the mayor in a mock election we had in 5$^{th}$ grade. I gave a speech in front of the whole class. In the end, I was elected. My English was not perfect yet, but I think faith and confidence gave me that success.

I remember God showing me a circular rainbow at the school in the morning on my first day at Conestoga Middle School. I tried my best in every subject. I played the clarinet and participated in several athletic activities, too. I also was active in the student council. One time I got a B in one of the subjects. I studied that subject intensely, and on the semester final I got an A in it. Through this experience, I gained more confidence with which I could do anything if only there was sufficient effort.

Three years after I went to the United States, in July 2009, I received mail from school. It was the President's Award for Academic Excellence. It recognizes academic success plus high achievement on state or nationally normed reading or mathematics examinations and recommendations of a teacher plus one other staff member. I got 4.0 GPA on a 4.0 scale all through my $6^{th}$ and $7^{th}$ grades, and I also received good results in the reading and mathematics exams conducted by the State of Oregon.

Q. How was your life in International School of Qingdao?

I didn't know any Mandarin or Chinese letters when I went there. But I studied Mandarin with patience just like when I had studied English. Now, I have improved to study HSK (Hànyǔ Shuǐpíng Kǎoshì – Chinese Proficiency Test) level 5.

I went to an American international school. In American schools all homework is reflected in the grade, so it is hard to get good grades if you neglect any of it. Sometimes I went to sleep at 3 AM after doing homework and studying. But I never thought it was hard nor did I give up studying. I just thought it is important to try hard in every matter.

In the classes I paid attention to the teacher and tried not to miss anything. If I didn't understand something, I asked questions until I understood them. Such an attitude let me gain trust from the teachers, too.

### Q. What is your dream?

The sermon series on *'Secrets of Academic Excellence'* re-directed the course of my studying. I don't know much about the things most of my classmates are very interested in like popular songs, trends in fashion or popular TV shows.

But, when they ask me questions about their studies, I explain to them the best I can. I also participate in sports and other extracurricular activities, and it is good enough to earn the recognition and love from my classmates and seniors in school. I realized that all things go well when I try to be faithful in everything with faith.

I believe I will be able to get into the college I want and study the major I want if I keep on studying hard and try my best. Before I went to the United States, a pastor told me to study English and someday become great strength to the kingdom of God. I remembered his advice when I was studying. Even today I try my best to become a noble instrument for the kingdom of God.

# You Might be a Little Late, but Nothing is Impossible!

### Sister Bora Yoon

Majored in Dance at Seoul Christian College
Master's Degree in Korean Dance at Sejong University
Member of Heavenly Dance Team of Manmin Central Church

---

Whenever she performs, Bora Yoon dances with her love toward God. She began dancing at a relatively late age, and she'd like to share her experience with those who'd like to major in performing arts.

**Q. How did you come to major in dance?**

Toward the end of my junior year in high school I suddenly had the urge. My teacher said it was going to be very difficult for me to go to college as a dance major. Most dancers start dancing at a very young age, when they are kids. I understood what my teacher meant, that I wouldn't be able to compete with them. She said if I had to major in dance, maybe I'd have a chance for some low-level colleges located far from Seoul (In South Korea, most of the best universities are located in Seoul).

But I didn't want to go any of the colleges outside of Seoul because I was attending Manmin Central Church in Seoul. I finally gave up majoring in dance and decided to study food and nutrition.

But even in the college, my desire to give glory to God through dancing did not go away. I auditioned for one of the dancing teams in the church and was accepted. As I was practicing with other members, my desire to dance grew greater. So, I decided to take college entrance exam again to major in dance.

### Q. Since you started very late, how did you practice?

Of course I had to try much harder than others because I started late. I studied for the written exam in the morning and practiced dancing in the afternoon. I practiced two or three times more than my friends. Even on the way to the dancing school or whenever I had some space, I practiced the moves I had learned.

After the dancing school was over, I attended the Daniel prayer meeting, giving thanks to God that He guided me to dance. After the prayer was over, sometimes I'd study for the written exam again. If I felt I needed to practice more, I repeatedly practiced the same moves until I was good at it.

### Q. Wasn't it hard to study?

For such a process, many people might have thought it too difficult and given up in the same situation, but I couldn't. I had a clear goal that I'd give glory to God through dancing. I also believed that God would open a way for me to do that, and so I didn't feel it difficult at all.

I believed those friends who had started earlier were just a little bit ahead of me, and eventually we'd be standing at the same point. I just tried to focus and study. The circumstances were not all that good from the beginning for me to study dancing, but I convinced myself I would be able to do it with faith.

### Q. What are your future goals?

God saw that I didn't complain about the circumstances but just tried my best so that He let my dancing skills improve. He also opened a way for me to take the master's course in dancing so I could learn dancing more systematically.

Each graduate school has different criteria for selecting their students, and in case of Sejong University, they considered the written exam scores and the plans for the thesis, and there was an interview with the professor. It is God's grace that I was admitted to graduate school and came to learn dancing in more depth. I'd like to study and research more to be of help to those others who are learning dancing for God's glory.

# There Is No Mountain that I Can't Climb

**Deacon Minseok Seo**

M.D. Family Physician, Chung Ang University Hospital

Minseok Seo says the happiest times in his life are when he listens to the words of God. While listening to the sermons, all his questions are answered clearly. He also had difficulties until he became a medical doctor. But he overcame such difficulties and focused on studying. Let's hear his secrets.

Q. How did you raise your grades in high school?

The most important thing is the basics. In the first mock

exam I took in 10th grade, I didn't even get 40 out of 80 in math. I hated math and my fundamentals were weak in that subject.

So, after consulting with my teacher in the 11th grade, I decided to just keep on solving the problems for the 10th grade repeatedly. I became confident after I finished whole course for 10th grade four times. I think to lay the proper foundation is the key to raising the grades, even if it means you have to study the middle school courses again.

### Q. What was your favorite Bible verse while preparing for the entrance exam?

Sometimes you can't really focus on studying. At those times I listened to praise songs on the earphones. My mind would be cleared after about 10-20 minutes. Then, I could focus better, and I felt that God loved me.

Also, the verse, Philippians 4:13, *"I can do all things through Him who strengthens me,"* encouraged me while I was studying. For the three years in high school, my mock exam scores were never good enough to get into medical school. So, whenever I faced that reality, I brought the above verse into my remembrance, and then I felt strengthened.

Q. How did you balance religious life and studying?

I went to medical school because I thought I could evangelize more people while providing practical help to them. At first, when I was spending time in prayer, I was worried that I might fall behind other students.

But I just believed that God would help me, and I attended the Daniel prayer meeting held every night at the church. Also, as I studied after reading the Bible, God gave me grace to be able to concentrate more, so I could study a lot within a short period of time. Naturally I got good grades.

For the medial licensing exam, I received Rev. Jaerock Lee's prayer 100 days prior. He prayed that I would pass with a good grade and give glory to God. I had peace in my mind while preparing for it. I actually got more than enough score to pass. I also passed the exam for internship at Severance Hospital.

Q. Please give advice for students

I registered in Manmin Central Church during my third year of medical studies, and since then, I tried not to miss the

Daniel prayer meeting. Thanks to that effort, my grades went up to upper middle rank toward graduation. God leads us to good ways if we rely on Him without ceasing. I hope all the students will overcome each moment with patience.

In medical college, I felt like I was pouring water in a bottomless pot and the water drained right out of the bottom of the pot. I was disappointed in myself when I couldn't remember what I had just studied. But as I just kept on trying without giving up, my efforts began paying off.

You cannot just dig up the seed you've planted because you feel they aren't sprouting quickly enough. Why not just water them once again instead of digging them up? You will be able to bear much fruit eventually. Lastly, I'd like to recite the poem, 'Great Mountain'.

> "The Great Mountain is high, but is still under the sky.
> If one keeps on climbing, he will surely climb it.
> But people do not try to climb but just say, 'It is too high.'"

# To Give Everything, Not Just Half

**Brother Seungcheol Song**

Majored in Judo and Security at Yong In University

Seungcheol was raised in a Christian family. His sister had a heart condition that she should not have been able to overcome, but by the power of God she was healed completely. He gained faith seeing his sister recover. He had wandered around during his teens and caused his parents to be concerned a lot, but he is now setting an example for many teenagers. Here is how he spent his teen years in the grace of God and how he studied.

## Q. How were your teen years?

I was raised in a devout Christian family but I also had my period of 'teenage rebellion'. I liked hanging out with my friends more than being in the church or studying. I was drifting away from faith, but I still kept the Lord's Day and gave tithes regularly because I witnessed my baby sister getting healed by the power of God.

I was admitted to a middle school with a scholarship in soccer, but I quit playing because to continue playing meant I wouldn't be able to keep the Lord's Day. There was also an incident that took place around that time. On my way home from school, I heard some of my friends talk badly about my church. Being unable to control my temper for the moment, I punched them.

From the time of that incident I decided to become the strongest boy in the school. I went to the well-known fighters in the school and asked for a fight. Finally I became the 'number one' in the school. One day, I was wrongfully accused for what the students in another school did. After this incident, I decided to become the 'number one' among all the schools in the neighborhood. After going through several fights, I actually became the number one of several schools.

This news spread, and when I went to the high school, I automatically became the 'one' without having to fight. During the vacations, I didn't hang out with my friends just to concentrate on exercising. And during those times my friends won the fights against neighboring schools, and I became the 'boss' among more than 30 schools.

So, I was really a trouble-maker for my parents during my teens, but outside, I was happy because there were many friends who trusted and followed me. Naturally I started drinking and smoking. I was also into motor bikes and cars. Knowing all these things, my parents just waited with faith and love. Because I knew my parents' love, I tried to turn from my ways but I did not have the strength to do it.

Somehow I got into college and then I had to do my military duty. Rather than the fear of hard military training, suddenly I became afraid that I might go to Hell. Because my parents were leaders in the church, I was ashamed to meet with the senior pastor of my church, Rev. Jaerock Lee. But I honestly talked about my faults with him and with a repenting heart I received his prayer. He asked how hard it must have been for me all those years, and prayed for me earnestly, advising me not to look at the world again. That meeting with him and his prayer enabled me to get back on the right track.

## Q. Was there a special reason you decided to study?

In my teens I didn't study at all. It's just that I never felt the need for it. But as my military duty was coming to an end, I began to think about my future and what I could do. As I was praying about my future, I remembered my childhood dream. I once thought the security team, the bodyguards looked 'cool' and I wanted to be one of those people.

Once I remembered that dream, I wanted to become a member of the security team for the President at Cheong Wa Dae, which is the presidential palace of South Korea. Their pre-requisites were not just about martial arts. I had to take exams in English, social studies, economics, politics, law, and science, which are the exams for grade 7 civil workers. So I decided to study and began with studying English.

## Q. Did you have any special method in studying?

Because I never studied during my teens, all I knew in English was just the alphabet. Drowsiness engulfed me as soon as I opened the book. But thankfully, some of my juniors in the military were from the most prestigious universities, and I got their help.

First, I decided on the hours of studying. I tried to keep those hours no matter what. I never gave up even though I couldn't understand the contents. Even while I was in field training, I read the books with lanterns late at night.

When there was a lot of training we had to do, I volunteered to work in the early morning so I could study in the evening. I just wanted to do all my best and commit the results to God. As I kept on studying that way for a couple of months, I gradually began to understand what the English language is like.

I believed the hours invested in studying and exercising were times offered to God's kingdom, and God gave me ability to focus and concentrate. He let me gain more things than I could have acquired on my own, and He guided me to the quickest and best ways. Within a year after I got out of the military, I could teach martial arts to foreigners in English. In school my grades were at the bottom but in college, I was at the top of my class. I was even getting scholarships, too.

While I was keeping my study hours, I kept my prayer time as well. When the exams were coming up, I did not reduce the hours of prayer to study more. I prayed with all my heart to rely on God. I prayed to give me the power of concentration so I could cover all the materials needed for the exams, although my studying hours might only be half of those of others.

I thought he who reduces the praying hours is relying on their own ability more than on God. And in fact, God let me get the grades to be one of the highest in class when I prayed more to rely on God. One time, I just opened the book and briefly read some materials just 10 minutes before the exam, and those things were actually in the exam.

## Q. What is your future goal?

One of the most important principles for a bodyguard is to make the client feel at ease. But as for me, for the security of the church members, I think the first thing for a security staff member is to cultivate the heart of spirit. So, whenever I realized something that had to be changed in me, I fasted and offered vowed prayers.

Listening to the message titled, "Plow Your Heart-field" I realized all of the thorns, rocks, and the roadside in my heart. But I was happy to hear that the sinful natures will be burned away by the fire of the Holy Spirit through fervent prayers. Since then, I prayed about the things of the flesh I had realized within me in my daily life. As I kept on praying that way, I could feel that I was beginning to change.

I am also challenged seeing the brothers in faith around me. They give thanks to God in situations that are incomparably harder than mine. And I ask myself, "Am I living for the kingdom of God with all my best?"

To cultivate the heart of spirit that is free of evil is the first step, and I should also have physical abilities, too. I will try harder until all my dreams come true. I will just go on giving God all my heart and not just the half of it.

# Make Your Own Way, Not Just Your 'Profile'

Elder Youngshik Hong

Majored in Chemistry at Korea University
PhD in Science, Korea University
Professor of Science Education at Seoul National University

Elder Youngshik Hong received his PhD degree at the age of 32. After he worked as a researcher at the University of Bordeaux in France for two years, he came back to South Korea and worked as the head researcher at Korea Electronics and Communications Research Center. In 2005, he became a professor at Seoul University of Education. In his childhood, he thought teachers who were on good terms with their students seemed very nice and he wished to be such a teacher. Now his dream came true. Let us hear from him how he accomplished his childhood dream.

Q. Was there a special occasion where you decided to really study?

My parents wanted me to become a scholar or a diplomat. It was difficult to get into good schools in the countryside, so from 6$^{th}$ through 8$^{th}$ grade, I lived at my uncle's house which was 40km away from home.

I went home during the weekends, and took the first bus on Monday morning to go to school. Seeing my parents waving their hands through the bus windows, I made up my mind to study hard. This determination did not waver until I finished my undergraduate work and then received a Master's degree. Eventually I pursued further studies to get a PhD degree.

Q. Tell us about your doctorate studies and how you became a professor.

The most difficult thing during my doctorate program was uncertainty for the future. I was in a disadvantageous position because I got my degree in South Korea, and not from more famous universities abroad. So I tried harder to compensate for that handicap. In 1997, the year I received my PhD degree, I published six theses that were put on SCI (Science Citation Index). After the doctorate program, I went to France to study abroad for two years, and then for a short time I worked as a researcher at Korea University.

After that I came to work for the Korea Electronics and Communications Research Institute located in Daejeon. I was doing a research work in the field of inorganic chemistry, which was my major. Many times I thought I needed more time for my research, but I still sought God's kingdom and His righteousness first (Matthew 6:33). I was the president of the Men's Mission in Daejeon Manmin Church, and my priority was always saving the souls.

As I tried my best in my research while working faithfully for the kingdom of God, He gave me wisdom and understanding and I achieved a lot of things in my research. I wrote 51 theses by 2005. After that, by God's grace and blessing I was hired as a professor at Seoul University of Education. At last my dream came true as a professor.

Q. What do you think students need to do to achieve their dreams?

I believe the most important thing in achieving your dream is endurance and effort. Once, an American psychologist, Terman, studied 1,528 children who had 140+ IQs after they had grown up. He found that their lives were not so different from those of ordinary people. Why? It's because they didn't try harder than others.

I believe the key to success is your efforts rather than the innate talents. During my Master's and Doctorate programs, I couldn't see my future but I did not give up midway. I just kept on studying and researching to achieve my dream.

Q. How do you suggest students choose a major and a university?

What is more important than the popularity of a particular major or the possibility of getting a job after graduating from a particular university is how good you can become in a chosen field/major. Everybody has a field in which they are good at. Choosing a university is important, but I'd say choosing a major is more important. Not everyone succeeds just because they got into prestigious universities. Even though you can't get accepted by a particular university due to your grades, it doesn't mean at all that you will fail in the future.

Up until the high school, you need to do well in all subjects, but from college, you can choose the major that you can do the best, and you can excel as you keep on working. Anybody can achieve their dream by trying their best, no matter which university you are studying at.

## Q. What is your advice for students now?

Oftentimes I tell the students a story of two friends, Gilbert and Tom. They were classmates in high school. Gilbert was always at the top of his class. Tom was just ordinary. Later they went to the same college and studied the same major. Gilbert was quite disappointed at his performance and did not study hard any longer, but Tom tried even harder. Soon, Tom began to exceed Gilbert in academic performance.

Gilbert always said, "I can do better once I begin." But he never began. Tom is a professor at a prestigious university in South Korea after studying in the United States. Your grades in middle school or high school might not be so impressive. But you can begin now. Psalm 126:5 says, *"Those who sow in tears shall reap with joyful shouting."* If you just keep trying in a particular area, you can become an expert in that field. It's not too late if you begin in middle school, high school, or in college. Of course, the sooner the better! Success is proportionate to the time invested, and it is a fruit of faithfulness.

# I Could Overcome Anything Dreaming about the Future

**Brother Jay Yoon Kim**

Studying at Irvine Valley College, California

Jay received the President's Award for Academic Excellence in June 2010. He says he was happy that his efforts paid off. He says, "Never give up. Have faith that you can do everything with the help of God. Try your best on homework and tests. Ask the teachers whenever you need help. Be humble enough to learn from your friends."

Q. How did you happen to study in the United States?

In 2000, when I was 9 years old, my whole family

immigrated to Las Vegas. It was my father's decision that he had made after he experienced a great deal of spiritual thirst and limitations. We began a new life in a new environment, but he could not quench his spiritual thirst. Eventually, he began a 40-day vowed prayer for a spiritual turn-around.

One day, during his prayers, a certain name was echoing in his mind, which was "Jaerock Lee" but he did not realize that it was God's work. Later hearing this name so often in his mind, he began searching the Internet and came to know about Manmin Central Church.

As he was listening to the sermons on 'Heaven' his vague feelings about the kingdom of heaven became more concrete, and as he was listening to the Lectures on Genesis, his spiritual thirst was being quenched. He wanted to listen to the sermons so much, even to the extent that he couldn't get to sleep because he wanted to find out what was in the next sermon.

Q. How did you spend your teen years?

I didn't really like studying in middle school. I loved hanging out with my friends much more than studying.

Sometimes I hung out with bad friends and did mischievous things, too. Once I was addicted to computer games. I spent all day playing games in a park instead of going to school. Naturally my grades began to fall.

But then, suddenly, a thought flashed through my mind. It was, "Where would I go if I die now?" I felt I was going to Hell. I came to my senses that I couldn't live the way I had done any longer. Realizing that I needed to change my life, I repented of all the past wrongdoings. In particular, I threw out all the games and decided to study.

My parents were very happy with the change and provided a lot of support, especially with prayers. I began to change while I was reading the Bible. Then, listening to the sermons of Rev. Jaerock Lee, I came to have a lot of pangs of conscience. I realized in detail and specifically how evil my heart was.

Since then, I tried not to speak of evil things and not to judge or condemn anybody. I tried to stretch out my hands to those who were neglected and in need around me and spread the gospel to them. When I was in the $7^{th}$ and $8^{th}$ grade, I tried to become a born-again, true Christian and tried my best to spread the gospel.

Q. Do you have any secrets of studying?

Before my life began to come around, I didn't have any desire to study. But after listening to the holiness gospel, I realized that God is pleased when I fulfill the duty as a student. I wanted to give glory to God by studying hard.

I didn't begin to study until reading the Bible and asking God for wisdom. I could feel that God was helping me understand the classes better. When I didn't understand something in the class, I always asked my teacher questions about it until I understood it completely. As I kept on doing the previews and reviews of the classes every day, I realized that studying was easy and fun. When I didn't feel like studying, I endured thinking about myself in the future. That eased my mind and I could study again.

My first secret to raising grades was to pray to God. God is the source of wisdom. When I prayed to give me heavenly wisdom, God let me focus and have the ability to understand the class better. The second secret is to imagine myself in the future. I wanted to be a person who would be competent and capable of any given task. Even though it was hard to study, a clear vision and dream helped me get through those hard times. My grades increased dramatically through these methods.

## Q. How did you get the President's Award for Academic Excellence?

The standards for the President's Award are slightly different from state to state. In Nevada, they present it at the graduation of elementary school, middle school, and high school. Of course the first criterion is the grades. One must achieve a grade point average of 3.5 or higher in every semester. There are many other things that they consider, too. The student must participate and excel in extracurricular activities, too, and there must be recommendation of a teacher.

I received the President's Award at the high school graduation. I was the president of a Christian group in the school for four years, vice president of the recycling group for two years, president of math group for two years, and a member of National Honor Society for three years, and a band member as a clarinetist for three years. I also made a missionary trip to Peru in 2007, and I believe all these activities counted in the consideration for the Award.

Q. Any advice to the students preparing for college entrance?

I want to say it'd be best if they prepare for the SAT at an early stage. If they study for it in the senior year of high school, it will be too late. They should lay firm foundations at least from the freshman year and understand everything in each subject so they can study the next courses more easily.

I also want to say that they need to pay attention in the classes. Without paying attention in the class, it's not going to be easy even if you study extra hours. Classes in the school must be thoroughly learned. Lastly, I ask them to please God. Have fellowship with God through prayer at a designated time every day, and spread the gospel to friends. They also need to catch the message that God is giving to them while meditating on the Bible.

Q. What is your future plan?

I was accepted by Boston University with financial aid

amounting to 80% of the tuition, but I chose Irvine Valley College in California with a chemistry major, in order to help with the ministry of my father. My dream is to become a professor in mathematics, teaching the students and sharing the gospel with many people.

So, as for now, I'd like to focus on my studies and especially on math studies. My short-term goal is to transfer to UC Berkeley with mathematics major. I am also doing my best in all areas as a tutor for college students, Christian students' club, and a member of the student government.

## The Author
## Dr. Jaerock Lee

Dr. Jaerock Lee was born in Muan, Jeonnam Province, Republic of Korea, in 1943. While in his twenties, Dr. Lee suffered from a variety of incurable diseases for seven years and awaited death with no hope for recovery. However one day in the spring of 1974 he was led to a church by his sister and when he knelt down to pray, the living God immediately healed him of all his diseases.

From the moment he met the living God through that wonderful experience, Dr. Lee has loved God with all his heart and sincerity, and in 1978 he was called to be a servant of God. He prayed fervently with countless fasting prayers so that he could clearly understand the will of God, wholly accomplish it and obey the Word of God. In 1982, he founded Manmin Central Church in Seoul, Korea, and countless works of God, including miraculous healings, signs and wonders, have been taking place at his church ever since.

In 1986, Dr. Lee was ordained as a pastor at the Annual Assembly of Jesus' Sungkyul Church of Korea, and four years later in 1990, his sermons began to be broadcast in Australia, Russia, and the Philippines. Within a short time many more countries were being reached through the Far East Broadcasting Company, the Asia Broadcast Station, and the Washington Christian Radio System.

Three years later, in 1993, Manmin Central Church was selected as one of the "World's Top 50 Churches" by the *Christian World* magazine (US) and he received an Honorary Doctorate of Divinity from Christian Faith College, Florida, USA, and in 1996 he received his Ph. D. in Ministry from Kingsway Theological Seminary, Iowa, USA.

Since 1993, Dr. Lee has been spearheading world evangelization through many overseas crusades in Tanzania, Argentina, L.A., Baltimore City, Hawaii, and New York City of the USA, Uganda, Japan, Pakistan, Kenya, the Philippines, Honduras, India, Russia, Germany, Peru, Democratic Republic of the Congo, Israel and Estonia.

In 2002 he was acknowledged as a "worldwide revivalist" for his powerful ministries in various overseas crusades by major Christian newspapers in Korea. In particular was his 'New York Crusade 2006' held in Madison Square Garden, the most famous arena in the world. The event was broadcast to 220 nations, and in his 'Israel United Crusade 2009', held at the International Convention Center (ICC) in Jerusalem he boldly proclaimed Jesus Christ is the Messiah and Savior.

He was listed as one of the 'Top 10 Most Influential Christian Leaders' of 2009 and 2010 by the popular Russian Christian magazine *In Victory* and news agency *Christian Telegraph* for his powerful TV broadcasting ministry and overseas church-pastoring ministry.

As of the date of this publishing, Dr. Lee has written 113 books,, including bestsellers *Tasting Eternal Life before Death, My Life My Faith I & II, The Message of the Cross, The Measure of Faith, Heaven I & II, Hell, Awaken, Israel!,* and *The Power of God*. His works have been translated into more than 76 languages.

Dr. Lee is currently leader of many missionary organizations and associations. Positions include: Chairman, The United Holiness Church of Jesus Christ; Permanent President, The World Christianity Revival Mission Association; Founder & Board Chairman, Global Christian Network (GCN); Founder & Board Chairman, World Christian Doctors Network (WCDN); and Founder & Board Chairman, Manmin International Seminary (MIS).

Other powerful books by the same author

### Heaven I & II

A detailed sketch of the gorgeous living environment the heavenly citizens enjoy and beautiful description of different levels of heavenly kingdoms.

### The Message of the Cross

A powerful awakening message for all the people who are spiritually asleep! In this book you will find the reason Jesus is the only Savior and the true love of God.

### Hell

An earnest message to all mankind from God, who wishes not even one soul to fall into the depths of hell! You will discover the never-before-revealed account of the cruel reality of the Lower Grave and Hell.

### My Life My Faith I & II

Dr. Jaerock Lee's autobiography provides the most fragrant spiritual aroma for the readers, through his life extracted from the love of God blossomed in midst of the dark waves, cold yoke and the deepest despair.

### The Measure of Faith

What kind of a dwelling place, crown and reward are prepared for you in heaven? This book provides with wisdom and guidance for you to measure your faith and cultivate the best and most mature faith.

### Spirit, Soul, and Body I & II

A guidebook that gives the reader spiritual understanding of spirit, soul, and body, and helps him find what kind of 'self' he has made so that he can gain the power to defeat darkness and become a person of spirit.

### Awaken Israel!

Why has God kept His eyes on Israel from the beginning of the world to this day? What kind of His providence has been prepared for Israel in the last days, who await the Messiah?

### Seven Churches

The letter to the seven churches of the Lord in the book of Revelation is for all the churches that have existed up until now. It is like a signpost for them and a summary of all the words of God in both Old and New Testaments.

### Footsteps of the Lord I & II

An unraveled account of secrets about the beginning of time, the origin of Jesus, and God's providence and love for allowing His only begotten Son Passion and resurrection!

### The Power of God

A must-read that serves as an essential guide by which one can possess true faith and experience the wondrous power of God

www.urimbooks.com

www.ingramcontent.com/pod-product-compliance
Lightning Source LLC
LaVergne TN
LVHW041703060526
838201LV00043B/558